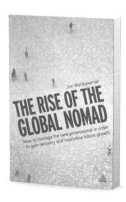

The Rise of the Global Nomad

The Rise of the Global Nomad

How to manage the
new professional in
order to gain recovery
and maximize future
growth

Jim Matthewman

KoganPage

LONDON PHILADELPHIA NEW DELHI

Publisher's note

Every possible effort has been made to ensure that the information contained in this book is accurate at the time of going to press, and the publishers and author cannot accept responsibility for any errors or omissions, however caused. No responsibility for loss or damage occasioned to any person acting, or refraining from action, as a result of the material in this publication can be accepted by the editor, the publisher or the author.

First published in Great Britain and the United States in 2011 by Kogan Page Limited

120 Pentonville Road	1518 Walnut Street, Suite 1100	4737/23 Ansari Road
London N1 9JN	Philadelphia PA 19102	Daryaganj
United Kingdom	USA	New Delhi 110002
www.koganpage.com		India

© Jim Matthewman, 2011

ISBN   978 0 7494 6015 0
E-ISBN   978 0 7494 6016 7

British Library Cataloguing-in-Publication Data

A CIP record for this book is available from the British Library.

Library of Congress Cataloging-in-Publication Data

Matthewman, Jim.
    The rise of the global nomad : how to manage the new professional in order to gain recovery and maximize future growth / Jim Matthewman.
        p. cm.
    ISBN 978-0-7494-6015-0 – ISBN 978-0-7494-6016-7 (ebook) 1. Diversity in the workplace. 2. Intergenerational relations. 3. Generation Y–Management. I. Title.
    HF5549.5.M5M38 2011
    658.3008–dc22
                                                                                    2010042007

Typeset by Saxon Graphics Ltd, Derby
Production managed by Jellyfish
Printed in the UK by CPI Antony Rowe

Dedications

To Suzi, my wife, and our Generation Y children,
Miles and Gemma.
Also in loving memory of my parents, Barbara and Gerald,
who took me off to Arabia, aged seven.

CONTENTS

PREFACE

W hy is this book important and who should be reading it?

A Workspan study (3 March 2010) has stated that the world's mobile workforce will pass 1 billion in 2010 and will rise by 20 per cent to 1.2 billion by 2013. Most significantly, most will be based in the Asia-Pacific region.

There are new multicultural, global professionals in the market. They can accelerate growth for multinationals and aspiring international firms. For many organizations, this group may only be 10 to 15 per cent of their total workforce but they are hugely impactful, some CEOs saying they directly contribute 20 per cent of total revenue and an even higher proportion of profit. They are predominately younger professionals (Generations X and Y, who have strong support from a parental Baby Boomer, ie the generation aged 50 plus) and will drive results, growth and the next wave of profitability from the emerging markets.

This is key. The evidence is undeniable. Recovery and growth will take a long time in the traditional mature markets; the real action is happening in the emerging markets. The global nomads are the vanguard of this shift towards the East; they can make the connections and they have the enthusiasm and energy to lead the challenge.

CEOs and senior human resources directors of multinationals need to attract, engage and motivate this relatively small group fast, as everybody is seeking them out.

So primarily this is a wake-up call for multinational CEOs: their current people strategies are out of step and whilst these predominately Western organizations are spending substantial effort in retrenchment, reviewing process, systems and cost, there is another market out there which new, regionally based competitors are homing in on.

The underlying people strategies of the multinational firms need review and to tune into a new heartbeat that will require a new way of working, a new employment deal and a reassessment of performance and talent management.

The second group of readers is the global nomads themselves. Their personal views, expectations and aspirations have been collated in this book through 100 personal interviews. This is the first time this has been done. The nomads show clear traits, wonderful optimism and a rich stream of passion, professionalism and ambition – way beyond their peers in mature markets. However, they need a dose of realism to see how organizations will respond to the recovery. But the message is clear from the selected group of corporate interviews in Part Five of the book: the global nomads are in a sellers' market – a significant shift is occurring that will impact over the next 10 years, and they are uniquely placed for it.

The next group is the executives and senior managers of the multinationals (ie the Baby Boomers, aged 50 plus), who will resonate with the personal insights of this new breed in their own Generation X and Generation Y offspring. How will the global labour market react to their children entering the professional world? This is the question that frequently arises in my lectures all around the world.

Finally there is the wider public, which includes partners, families and friends of the rapidly growing group of global nomads. Most of these people are quick to acknowledge this new group of employees – in fact, everyone knows one. So quite deliberately this book is written on a number of levels; it is not an academic text; hopefully it is a readable management book to be read on trains, planes and even beaches, and will attract the curiosity of wives, husbands and the Generation X and Y offspring of globally nomadic parents.

My conclusion is that this is a new employment trend that will multiply exponentially. The opportunity is huge. Savvy employers should review the profiles and use this knowledge to actively seek out these new nomads – they are a small group but, it seems, one that everybody will want.

I sincerely hope that you will enjoy reading this book. If you have personal insights, perspectives or comments, please do not hesitate to contact me at **jim.matthewman@gmail.com**.

ACKNOWLEDGEMENTS

With over 27 years of consulting to more than 2,500 organizations in 36 countries with hundreds of colleagues, impacting literally millions of employees, I have a potential list of thousands of people to acknowledge. Every organization and everybody has had a story to tell – which is why I have one of the best jobs in the world.

This book is about a special subset of the workforce and their expectations, which are the vanguard to a new breed of workers who will become the engine room of tomorrow and are already helping to shape the global economic recovery.

In preparing this book I specifically looked at the nomads in Dubai. The city grew on a wave of petrodollars to diversify into three other industry sectors – financial services, real estate and high-class tourism – only to find all three taking a hammering as a result of the economic crisis. But Dubai's issues are minor compared with national debts in the mature economies. With the huge funds and reserves located in the UAE and other Gulf states, its ambitions have not been dulled. Dubai is truly remarkable as the first modern city to be built primarily for expats. It is a fantasy town but you can touch it. It is transient, like many of its inhabitants, but at the same time is proving to be sustainable as the region's transport hub. The book includes detail of the lives, expectations and ambitions of 50 global nomads in Dubai, of whom 35 are colleagues of mine in Mercer's Dubai office. That office is remarkable. We have 50 consultants from 29 different nationalities. Most are under 30, have a Master's or MBA, and speak on average three or four languages. They display a vibrancy, energy and commitment unlike anything I have seen elsewhere. To everyone in the office and those interviewed, a very special thank you.

In addition, there were another 15 nomads in Dubai of different ages and from varied professions: construction engineers, marketers, a web designer, oil and gas service contractors, bankers, aircrew, real-estate, HR and IT professionals. Going further afield, I interviewed a further 50 expats who are consultants, investment bankers, investors, medical researchers, environmentalists, oil workers, hotel executives, industrialists, production engineers and civil engineers or retirees in Hong Kong, Mumbai, Singapore, Shanghai, Sydney, London and New York. Some were new acquaintances who were intrigued by the subject matter, and some were dear friends scattered across the globe. More heartfelt thanks.

The important feedback I gleaned right from the start was at any professional dinner, party or the many conferences and seminars I gave, nearly everyone resonated with the idea and personally knows a global nomad.

Then there are the CEOs and senior vice presidents or group HR directors from 12 leading organizations who shared their viewpoints on the impact of the recovery and their insight into the future workforce. A huge thanks to these people for their willingness to participate and for their valuable time and foresight of why the new workforce is so important: true signs of the leadership required to steer us ahead.

Given all my travels, I am clearly a nomad – flying somewhere nearly every other week, and it is not done yet. There is still a lot to see, listen to and do. It is not all glamorous – it can be incredibly stressful, can be hugely frustrating, has massive implications for family life, yet at the same time is immensely rewarding.

Special thanks, of course, to Mercer and my various leaders, mentors and worldwide colleagues of many years who have encouraged these efforts. Special mention needs to made of David and Ginny Barford, Sue Filmer, Andrzej Narkiewicz, Cameron Hannah, Steve Faigen, Martin Meerkerk, Josy Koumans, Mike Piker and Chris Johnson for their active support in completion of the book.

Finally, there have been some amazing personal assistants – Katrina Stark, Elizabeth Protheroe and Chrissy Fisher – who have had to juggle appointments, changes in flight schedules, emergency visa applications, rearranging personal commitments throughout. I did say it would never be boring.

Next is Miles, my Generation Y son, whom I thank for assisting with the mobility research, for interviewing nomads in Dubai, for his generational insights, and for being a great reality check.

Most of all, I must thank my wife, Suzi, who has endured years of nights away from home, last-minute changes to family plans, calls at ridiculous times given varied time zones, and a life of constant flux. Much love always.

FIGURES

TABLES

PART ONE
The source of recovery

Introduction

There is an urgent need for new thinking – a clear mind shift – in terms of leadership and people management as the focus of world recovery switches from US and Western best practices to recovery and growth centred on Middle and Far Eastern economies.

A new cadre of global professionals is appearing who will drive both the recovery and future growth of international organizations. This group of professionals is focused on a multicultural, people-centred way of doing business in the emerging and developing countries. But they are not the traditional expats – a new latitudinal mobility is replacing the longitudinal assumptions of the past. This new group are the global nomads.

These professionals move from assignment A to assignment B, C and D over a period of 10 to 12 years and as such they are not expats who fly out from a home base and then fly back again. They do not have a 'home location'. This group is comfortable with change and sees each assignment as the source of challenge and new experience. The implications of this change are huge in terms of people management and the leadership challenges they pose. It actually reflects an opportunity of doing business in a completely different way with a new workforce reflecting international and regional mindsets rather than outdated Western views of globalization.

Current leadership, talent and performance management as well as reward programmes will need to change. Aggressive targets fuelled by excessive short-term bonus cultures for a few have lost the trust of the workers. Can employees really believe that the business and political leaders who created the worst global recession for 75 years have the vision and leadership to engage a new workforce? The nomads are unlikely to commit to 10 to 15 years of loyalty to a single firm but expect to see organizations offer opportunities and experiences rather than a career based on grade progression and tenure. The new organizational systems will be people-based networks – a sort of commercial Facebook built on who you know internally and externally rather than set structures with controlling reporting lines. And it is already happening.

FIGURE 0.1 Global GDP growth (percentage, quarter over quarter, annualized)

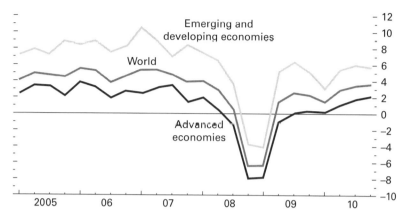

SOURCE: IMF[1]

The current financial and economic recession has had a profound impact on world business although some trends were already emerging.

Organizations and their business leaders are now focused on stabilization and cost reduction – 'right-sizing' the workforce is top of the agenda. Loss of jobs, cuts in pay and low job security have undermined the fragile relationship between employees and their companies. Combined with apparent payouts for failure to former CEOs and senior executives, the future will require a different employment proposition.

Some signs of green shoots are slowly appearing – Hong Kong is fast challenging New York and London as the world's leading city for banking and other financial services;[2] chip makers and PC manufacturers are no longer sending workers home; the major telecom firms are searching out new acquisitions; but this is all happening east of Cairo.

The world is already different post-Lehman; the US–European dominance has collapsed and organizations are already looking east. Key talent and key resources are being moved to pockets of business activity, notably the developing and emerging markets of the Middle East and the Far East, with the knowledge that organizations need to be ahead of the curve as these economies will break out of the global recession first and more strongly than the West. However, there is one exception of note: Brazil. Whilst Russia, in contrast, focused too strongly on energy rather commodities and as such was hit much harder by the global crisis than India or China, Brazil's recent oil strikes are leading some economists to predict it will become the 'New Middle East'. Unlike Russia, whose focus on commodities rather than products and services, coupled with a chronic lack of managerial and specialist professional talent, has restricted recovery. Projections suggest three of the top four economies in the next 25 years will be Asian.[3] Three of the world's four largest banks by market value are now Chinese.[4]

Regionalization, not the former US mantra of globalization, is the new business philosophy with more understanding and acceptance of local markets, local diversity and local ways of working. This will create a much more flexible approach to employment and deployment of labour. The much touted Western management frameworks and business practices will need to be tempered and tailored to maximize opportunities.

And the workforce is changing fast: the rightsizing and economic forecast of upturn will see Generation Y (those born after 1983) as the new engine room of the workforce. Whilst CEOs and organizations recognize that they need to adapt their profit models and employment strategies to embrace the energy, values and phenomenal potential of this new breed, Generation Y has also felt the chill of recession. How will they react?

With all this change, it will require a new set of leaders capable of handling this turmoil and who are more agile and prepared to grasp change and the new opportunities but with a much keener focus on new business development and execution. A massive step change is required – this needs to start with multinational CEOs and their top teams. Many are questioning whether the political and corporate leaders who led us into the global recession can really be the people to lead us out.

Finally, many organizations had set themselves bold visions and reform campaigns to be realized in 2010, unaware of the forthcoming collapse of the global economy. So with this chastening, this book has asked 12 multinational business leaders to share their predictions of what 2015 will bring – how much change will we see in the world of work and where?

This book is based on conversations over the past five years in particular with companies, delegates at lectures, friends and colleagues from around the world. What is clear is that global mobility is rising rapidly. Within professional social circles nearly everyone knows at least one global nomad, irrespective of age or location.

The backbone of the book is centred on the Middle East, where I have worked extensively and where I now live, in Dubai. Part of this is because Dubai is a unique city in the world. It is the first that has been built for global nomads: 85 per cent of its population is expatriate.[5] It has a fantasy atmosphere but one you can touch and feel – dreams have been made and lost here. Because its population is also transient, there is a constant ebb and flow of individuals passing through not just as tourists but at given points of their working life. It is has provided a starting point in comparing how other major cities, such as Hong Kong, London, New York, Singapore, Sydney and Shanghai, act as talent hubs.

References

1 IMF (2009) 'Sustaining the recovery', *World Economic Outlook*, Volume 2009, Number 2, October, p 30
2 'Hong Kong nears financial top spot', Brooke Masters, *Financial Times*, 20 September 2010
3 Ibid
4 www.bloomberg.com/apps/news?pid=20601109&sid=aueh06DOY37A
5 globalisation.inquirer.net/news/breakingnews/view/20080224-120926/ Influx-of-expats-boosts-UAE-population-report

The impact of the economic crisis

01

The economic and financial crisis following the crash of Lehman Brothers in September 2008 has fundamentally changed the world. The implosion of the financial systems in the United States and the UK rapidly spread to all markets around the world, requiring huge injections of public funds to stabilize local and world economies. The size of these fiscal stimuli worldwide has exceeded $3 trillion as shown in Table 1.1.

However, the impact of the crisis and subsequent recession was not even – some markets were not as exposed as others to fragile linkages between financial markets, credit exposure, housing prices and consumer demand. In the United States and the UK these linkages were highly related with the effect that major banks, insurance firms and retailers were jointly affected in rapid succession.

The result was that governments in the United States, UK, Europe and then Asia had to react by taking control of the financial markets through emergency regulation, partial or full ownership of major companies, tax cuts, spending on infrastructure, building projects and lowering interest rates.

Most economies did get caught up in the financial maelstrom as stock markets around the world responded to massive falls in New York, London and Frankfurt. Some of the new emerging markets, especially in Eastern Europe and Asia – Armenia, Georgia, Hungary, Iceland, Latvia, the Ukraine and Pakistan – have had to seek support from the International Monetary Fund (IMF).

In the Middle East, whilst the show emirate of Dubai was shown to be exposed to the collapse of the financial markets, real estate and high-end tourism, as all three bore the brunt of the credit crisis. However, the impact on other markets, notably the six Middle Eastern states of Saudi Arabia, United Arab Emirates, Bahrain, Kuwait, Qatar and Oman (together known

TABLE 1.1 Fiscal rescue packages

	Total Fiscal Package (USD billions)	Total Fiscal Package as a Percentage of GDP in 2009	Likely Spending in 2009 (in USD billions)	Spending in 2009 as a Percentage of GDP
Argentina	13.2	3.9	13.20	3.9
Australia	26.5	2.5	11.66	1.1
Belgium	2.52	0.5	2.52	0.5
Brazil	3.6	0.2	3.60	0.2
Canada	31.06	2.0	15.53	1.0
Chile	4	2.3	4.00	2.2
China	586	13.0	257.84	6.1
France	32.75	1.1	33.00	1.1
Germany	103.3	2.8	44.42	1.2
Hungary	6.5	3.8	6.50	4.0
India	4	0.3	4.00	0.3
Indonesia	6.15	1.2	6.15	1.2
Italy	6.3	0.3	6.30	0.3
Japan	110	2.3	70.40	1.5
Korea	25	2.7	12.50	1.3
Malaysia	18.2	7.9	9.10	4.2
Mexico	54	4.7	22.14	1.9
Netherlands	7.56	0.8	7.56	0.8

	Total Fiscal Package (USD billions)	Total Fiscal Package as a Percentage of GDP in 2009	Likely Spending in 2009 (in USD billions)	Spending in 2009 as a Percentage of GDP
New Zealand	5	3.8	5.00	3.7
Norway	2.9	0.6	2.90	0.6
Philippines	6.84	3.7	3.42	1.3
Portugal	2.77	1.1	2.77	1.1
Russia	20	1.1	20.00	1.1
Saudi Arabia	60	11.3	21.00	4.0
South Africa	3.76	1.2	3.76	1.3
Spain	14.05	0.8	14.05	0.8
Switzerland	1.34	0.3	1.34	0.3
Thailand	8.32	2.8	3.16	1.2
Turkey	0	0.0	0.00	0.0
United Kingdom	36.36	1.3	33.81	1.2
United States	787	5.6	251.84	1.8
Vietnam	1	0.9	1.00	1.1
Total ($ billions)	1989.98		894.48	
Advanced Economies	1194.41		515.60	
Developing & Emerging Economies	795.57		378.87	

SOURCE: ILO *Stimulus Packages to Counter Global Economic Crisis: A review*[1]
2009 GDP based on IMF's growth forecasts for 2009

as the GCC – Gulf Cooperation Council), has been less marked or has been ring-fenced. In these states most of the wealth is still controlled within ruling families and their investment funds or state institutions, hence they were less exposed to investor or market forces. Of course, there were still spectacular losses and probably many that will never be admitted. In the case of China, the injection of some $586 billion[2] (the equivalent of 13 per cent of the country's GNP) has been used to shore up and rekindle consumer spending. China, with this injection and the country's insatiable drive, will still see projected growth of 8.5 per cent in 2009 and 10 per cent for 2010.[3] China's and India's economies were among a select few that managed to evade recession.

But these structural differences have meant, for example, that Saudi Arabia (with its huge cash reserves of around $128 billion) and Qatar (with its dominance in liquid gas production, where the prices did not collapse as much as oil) are now in strong positions to take advantage of any potential recovery and proverbial green shoots.

Indeed an article in *Newsweek* which quoted Goldman Sachs predicts that the shape of recovery will be heavily slanted towards the Asian economies. So by 2012 the three largest economies in the world will be China, Japan and India, not the United States or Europe.[4] So as Western economies shrank in 2009, those east of Cairo continue to grow, as shown in Table 1.2.

It is not just the volume but, significantly, the pace of growth. The debt in the United States and Europe is so huge that the recovery will be painfully slow. On 14 September 2009 – the anniversary of the Lehman Brothers bankruptcy – President Barack Obama referred to 'the need for Wall Street to enact the most ambitious overhaul of the financial system since the Great Depression', implying commitment to both his administration and regulatory reform. The UK's debt is expected to reach £1.4 trillion within five years, which will be a cost of over £31,000 per person in the UK, according to BBC calculations.[5] Recent predictions suggest it may take up to 10 years for the UK to return to its target growth rate.

China and the Middle East have become the new global investors, tabling and completing major acquisitions. Of these, China's interest in iron ore, coal and other mining has been critical. China is buying again and looking for power. It has concluded Australia's biggest export deal with Resourcehouse for coal and iron ore worth US$60 billion over the next 20 years.[6] China's Silosteel Corporation has also succeeded in its takeover bid for Australia's Midwest Group, in July 2009. Iran is wooing China for investment to cash into oil and gas development. Iran's oil ministry has announced investments of about $40 billion from China; the most recent, a consortium of Chinese and Japanese companies, has agreed a deal to develop oil facilities in Iran's Khuzestan province.[7] This has prompted the recovery in oil prices to over $70 per barrel,[8] which has meant that the Middle East senses a return of optimism. For example, Qatar has taken a 10 per cent stake in the luxury car firm Porsche and has agreed to create research, development and testing

TABLE 1.2 IMF: World economic outlook projections April 2010 (percentage change)[9]

Country	2007	2008	2009	2010
USA	2.0	1.1	−2.6	3.1
UK	2.6	0.7	−4.2	0.2
Euro area	2.7	0.8	−4.8	1.0
China	13.0	9.0	7.5	10.0
India	9.4	7.3	5.4	8.8
Brazil	5.7	5.1	−1.3	5.5
Middle East / N Africa	6.3	5.2	2.0	4.5

facilities in Doha.[10] All of this has confirmed a significant shift in both focus and balance of trade.

Last but not least have been spectacular oil finds in Brazil, where the Santos Basin potentially contains reserves of 80 billion barrels of oil, according to ANP estimates. If the discoveries are found to be commercially viable, it would catapult the country into a top-five exporter of oil. Car makers have also been attracted to Brazil's Camacai region. Here modern technology from one organization is being simultaneously linked to a Ford assembly plant: 'This is not just-in-time [production]; it is sequential delivery. Each component is made for a specific car. By making several models simultaneously we can maximize efficiency and supply mix of product that the consumer demands.'

The key message here is that the world has changed, its focus has shifted and emerging sources of trade are not only within countries primarily based between the tropics, but this power broking is not only with a weakened West but also between themselves. For example, Chevy – the Chinese car manufacturer – now has plants in Uruguay, Russia, Ukraine, Iran, Egypt, Indonesia and Malaysia.

Demographic changes

The second major influence creating the sea change is world demographics. Overall the world's population is predicted to grow by almost 400 million (5.68 per cent) in five years.[11] The pattern of growth has changed, as has the age profile within countries. The data in Figure 1.2 highlight the major change – one of declining population growth in the mature markets of Western Europe and the United States combining with a rapidly ageing

FIGURE 1.1 Demographic changes

Working-age population

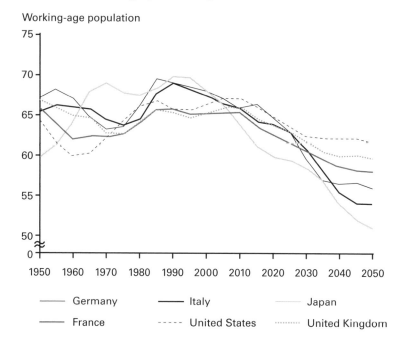

Old-age dependency ratio

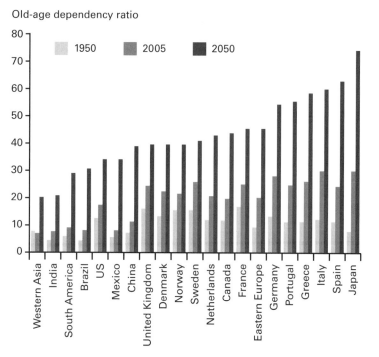

population, whilst many of the emerging countries are not only showing strong growth but a remarkably youthful shift. Within 10 years, India is forecasted to be the most populated country in the world, overtaking China.[12] Turkey, bidding to become the fourth-largest country by landmass and population in an expanded European Union, would be not only the first Muslim state but also the first to have 50 per cent of its population aged under 25.[13]

These data illustrate today's big issue of an ageing population in the mature economies but also a warning for the emerging markets that will surface over the next 40 years.

Population growth estimates suggest that by 2015, 95 per cent of the world's population will live within four hours' travel from Chennai, India. Furthermore, whilst India and China have fast-growing professional middle classes, both are outstripped by what is happening in Brazil.

In the past, demographic growth was hampered by availability of food and education. This, of course, remains true in large parts of the world – notably Africa, Central America and many Asian countries. Yet within the last 15 years, countries that were slow to change from post-World War II totalitarian regimes have experienced rapid transformation – including Croatia, the Baltics, Poland, Mexico, Vietnam, China, India, Malaysia, Egypt, Saudi Arabia and the UAE. Part of this has been driven by entrepreneurial modernity but also by huge advances in mass education, driven by better mathematics, computer and electronic technology plus widespread understanding of English, now generally accepted as the main business language the world over.

Radio, television and, most significantly, the internet have driven this thirst for knowledge, creating a desire to know about current events, cultural diversity, celebrities, world sport, music and the arts. The pace, availability and relatively low cost of mobile connectivity and visual images has meant that the world, for some people, has become a smaller place – although I personally view it as the opposite: a bigger place now available to more people with limitless opportunities, where technology can transcend borders connecting thousands, if not, millions of new groups of people. In 1969, over 600 million people worldwide witnessed Apollo 11 touching down and mankind walking on the moon.[14] In the 1980s and 1990s, mobile phone technology (it is believed that six in every 10 people of the world's population now own a mobile phone[15]) and popularization of the internet (360 million users by December 2000[16]) have revolutionized our ability to communicate across the world. Internet usage has spiralled to 1.7 billion users[17] (see Figure 1.3), with Windows Live Hotmail alone comprising over 270 million accounts.[18] The 2008 Beijing Olympics drew the world's largest television audience of all time, with an estimated 4.7 billion viewers. New Year's Eve 2008 recorded an astonishing 43 billion SMS messages sent globally.[19]

FIGURE 1.2 The internet

World Internet Users by World Regions

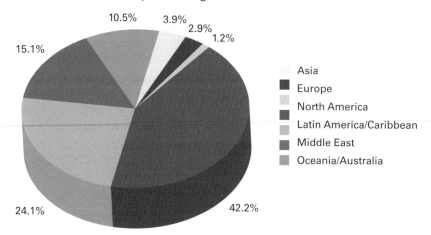

10.5%   3.9%
          2.9%
            1.2%
15.1%

24.1%   42.2%

- Asia
- Europe
- North America
- Latin America/Caribbean
- Middle East
- Oceania/Australia

SOURCE: Internet World Stats – **www.internetworldstats.com/stats.htm**
1,668,870,408 Internet users for June 30, 2009
Copyright © 2009, Miniwatts Marketing Group[20]

References

1 Sameer Khatiwada (2009) 'Stimulus packages to counter global economic crisis: a review', p 24, International Institute for Labour Studies, Geneva
2 ibid
3 IMF (2009) 'Sustaining the recovery', *World Economic Outlook*, Volume 2009, Number 2, October, p 162
4 *Newsweek*, February 2009
5 news.bbc.co.uk/2/hi/business/824834.stm
6 www.ft.com 'Resourcehouse in US$60 billion coal deal with China' by Peter Smith, 7 February 2010
7 www.thenational.ae,3.8.2009,tamsin.carlisle
8 www.thenation.com/doc/20091109/klare
9 IMF (2010) 'Rebalancing growth', *World Economic Outlook*, Volume 2010, April
10 *The National*, Sunday 16 August 2009, Rebecca Bradhouse
11 US Census Bureau www.census.gov/ipc/www/idb/worldpop.php
12 www.census.gov/cgi-bin/broker
13 www.census.gov/ipc/www/idb/country.php Turkey population pyramid
14 Guinness World Records www.guinnessworldrecords.com/news/2008/02/080228.aspx
15 Based on data from International Telecommunication Union www.itu.int/ITU-D/icteye/Reporting/ShowReportFrame.aspx?ReportName=/WTI/CellularSubscribersPublic&ReportFromat=HTML4.0&RP_intYear=2008&RP_intLanguageID=1&RP_bitLiveData=False

16 www.internetworldstats.com/emarketing.htm

17 ibid

18 www.multichannel.com/article/134614-Beijing_Olympics_Sets_Gold_
   Standard_4_7_Billion_Global_Viewers.php

19 www.cellular-news.com/story/28496.php

20 www.internetworldstats.com/stats.htm

Generational change in the workplace

02

The pace of growth, in both population and popular technology, has also created societal and cultural change across generations. This has not only allowed new generations to challenge and develop their own ideas but also to embrace and brand the change through language, fashion, music, the arts and *how* the technology is used as their own. For the first time we now have a number of distinct generations co-existing yet claiming difference. Whilst there are some variations in era dates, for the purposes of this book my categorization is as follows: Traditionalists are those born before 1945, the Baby Boomers are those born between 1945 and 1960, Generation X are those born after 1960 and before 1983 and Generation Y are those born after 1983 and before 2000. These generational changes are key to understanding the psyche of the new nomads.

The Baby Boomers

Baby Boomers are the post-World War II children, ie those born after 1945 and before 1960. This generation was the first in the United States and Europe to have mass university education (25 per cent); they enjoyed the birth of rock and roll and permissive relations through 'the pill'. They also challenged the fighting in Vietnam, the atom bomb and press censorship, and set out an idealistic vision of one world linked by love. They were a generation whose parents drove them into lifetime professional careers based on loyalty to major corporates. But this dream of lifetime employment for their parents and themselves was shattered by the first post-war recession in the early 1980s.

The Baby Boomers were the first group in the mature economies to experience a significant period of world peace, relative economic and political stability and rapid growth in personal income and associated living standards. As children, this group were given a massive cloak of support from their parents who had endured so much pain and upheaval. Secondary education was revamped with a focus on mathematics, English and writing but also the introduction of foreign 'romance' languages, especially those based on Latin. This was to pave the way for European understanding and greater integration.

University education was opened up to the children of a growing middle class and for the first time countries like the UK saw the new generation attending college with the syllabi reflecting the growing interest in economic development, computing, plus new commercial courses such as marketing, business studies and wider 'worldly subjects' such as humanities.

But university education in the 1960s provided a lot more. For the first time post war, a group of late adolescents were able to review and challenge assumed doctrines and dogmas of established societies and their politicians. Universities taught aspiring undergraduates the importance of a 'balanced argument', looking at both sides of a dilemma. This freedom to challenge created a climate of alternative thinking and experimentation – a licence to push to the limits and challenge established societal rules and mores. For those in power this was a dangerous undercurrent of political unrest led by ungrateful, rebellious youth fuelled by a collapse of (military) discipline.

This nascent outflow of alternative thinking was united with the rise of a youth movement with new, provocative, bright fashion, new 'beat' music, permissiveness, and celebrities fashioned by the new media of radio and television. The latter provided a wider international window transcending national boundaries. The United States and Britain were the centres of the 'Swinging Sixties', driving a generation of outward-looking, free-speaking individuals.

This did, of course, boil over into political unrest – such as the Paris riots of 1968, CND (Campaign for Nuclear Disarmament) rallies, and most notably the anti-Vietnam War protests in the United States. Here was a generation being asked to sign up to a huge loss of life for causes they did not believe in and to fight a foe with no obvious endgame. Significantly, this is a theme that repeats itself for Generations X and Y with the wars in Iraq and Afghanistan.

Some may ask 'Is this really any different from previous generations in history?' Perhaps not in the sense of young men and women being forced to fight other nations, but for the Baby Boomers the difference was that international communications and media meant that the horrors of war (the iconic photograph of a Vietnamese girl burning with napalm) with less censorship made it easy to coalesce around a cause.

As a result, the Baby Boomers are an idealistic generation who, in the Woodstock vibe, believed the world could be saved – 'All you need is love.' It saw the fusion of flower power, psychedelia and spiritual karma with an outreach to Indian gurus, Hari Krishna monks, tie-dyes, loons and kitsch jewellery of the hippie lifestyle but with mod and rocker undertones. By the end of the 1960s and early 1970s, some of the earlier idealism had been lost through the assassinations of John and Robert Kennedy and Martin Luther King, and through political corruption at Watergate; however, this generation saw the birth of huge technology milestones in aircraft travel, colour television and the first man on the moon.

Surprisingly, for all of these counter-trends, this generation were told by their parents that they must get a university education and seek out a good job with one of the growing corporate conglomerates, such Procter & Gamble, Shell or Coca-Cola, which would guarantee career development and a job for life. If you earned your dues you would work your way up the grading structure to a corner office on a higher floor, plus the promise of increasing benefits, of which the most important was a company pension scheme to ensure financial security in retirement. Baby Boomers are most typically loyal workaholics searching out personal fulfilment whilst conforming to corporate values.

As a result, Baby Boomer professionals typically have longer tenure in given companies with some, notably civil servants or those working in former nationalized industries, never moving given the value of their defined benefit pension plans. Many will have an average of between eight and 10 years with a given employer and hence perhaps two or three employers over their lifetime employment.

Baby Boomers entered a world of work with an acceptance that the organization would determine their career development, provide relevant training and, in effect, plan out their lives. This also suited organizations, as they maintained control of reporting lines, employee expectations and were largely assured of employee loyalty.

As these organizations started to develop overseas operations, the notion of the modern expat was born. In truth, this practice of 'colonizing' overseas countries was something that state companies had done as far back as the previous century with organizations such as the East India Company. Those expats were most typically senior managers or executives sent out from head office to run local offices in established trading countries, often former colonies. These assignments were usually seen as a 'reward' for dedicated service and for trusted hands. The assignments were typically for a set period, usually three or four years, and were widely seen as analogous to a military tour of duty, generous in allowances and additional benefits and a clear step forward in a person's internal career with a clear expectation that, at some point, the employee would return to a significant position in headquarter leadership.

Generation X

Generation X are those who were born between 1960 and 1983. This group entered the world of work at the time of deregulation, a belief in market forces and rising prosperity born out of technology advances. This workforce pledged its loyalty to the new professions of IT, banking and professional services but less to a given firm. They are epitomized as the Yuppies (Young Upwardly Mobile Professionals) and Dinkies (Double Income No Kids Yet): career-seeking males and females focused on material gain and the accompaniments, ie fast cars, mobile phones and city apartments. They saw the introduction of the internet but also saw the dot.com bubble burst. However, the idea that anyone with talent could become a millionaire was born – witness David and Victoria Beckham, Madonna and Martha Fox.

Generation X, however, are very individually centred. Following the idealism of the Baby Boomers, this group are less trusting and more personally driven. As Figure 2.1 shows, their childhood saw rising divorce rates and many were brought up in broken families or by single parents. US and UK society was beginning to fragment with increased violent crime, rising street-level drug culture and heightened racial tensions such as the Brixton riots and the LA riots. Similar tensions were seen in France with the suburban riots at Les Minguettes near Lyon.

Wider geopolitical events also saw the fall of communism and the Berlin Wall, the Oklahoma City bombing, the Space Shuttle Challenger catastrophe, plus the worldwide outbreak of AIDS.

With this social tension, Generation X entering the workforce were given a different message. Corporates would no longer guarantee careers for life – this promise had been broken with the first post-war recession in 1981–82 when Generation X saw their parents being made redundant. Yet US and European market economics saw the rise of Margaret Thatcher and Ronald Reagan championing deregulation of the financial and commercial sectors. Computerization was also growing apace with IT, banking and professional services becoming the chosen occupations for recent graduates. Generation X were revelling in a world of rising materialism, miniaturization and availability of new gadgets such as car phones, Sony Walkmans and PCs.

As a result, Generation X are very self-reliant given that society was no longer willing or unable to provide a comfort zone. In response, Generation X are more cynical and distrusting of authority. But this generation is highly adaptive and entrepreneurial since they no longer relied on others, whilst becoming increasingly technology savvy.

In the world of work, Generation X became more mobile: not afraid of switching between employers within the same industry sector, as their loyalty lay with their personal brand. Generation X can be seen as 'Me plc' as they sought out money first (base pay and bonuses) plus any professional training and development on offer. This was the first generation to seek out immediate gratification and spending. The cult of consumerism prevailed.

FIGURE 2.1 Divorce rate, England and Wales

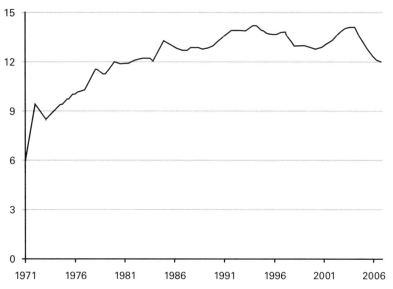

Persons divorcing per thousand married population

SOURCE: Office for National Statistics[1]

Easy credit became available and the spendthrift culture of the Traditionalists and Baby Boomers was lost. Professional success was measured in how long it took to double your salary. This was also the generation who drove the rise of the internet, the development of dot.com businesses, which could create overnight millionaires, and those who were prepared to risk it all – not just once, but a number of times.

Scarcity of key skills, notably specific computer application or hardware connectivity, new banking and electronic trading knowledge, plus specialist niche professional disciplines such as electronic engineering, desktop publishing, software engineering and web design all helped drive up salary rates for junior professionals. What people knew and how they could apply it were more important than years of experience. This scarcity of talent was fuelling a more mobile workforce – mainly within a country's borders but with a growing need across countries. Talent migration was starting to appear, especially migration to the technology centres and universities of Silicon Valley, Boston, Denver and Austin, Texas in the USA, the M4/M11 corridors in the UK, as well as Toulouse in France. However, these flows were primarily from certain European countries to the USA, UK or Japan.

Generation Y

Generation Y were born after 1983 – they are the 22- to 27-year-olds entering the workforce now. Some have labelled them the 'Echo Boomers', the 'Digital Generation' or the 'Millenniums'. They are exhibiting different values and behaviours than generations before them. They are incredibly confident, creative and worldly.

It is easy to say this is media hype, and history has shown there have always been generation clashes, for example the student riots in Paris in 1968. But this is different. The drive and energy of Generation Y are global, its members are green and put work into a social context whereby they no longer live for work (the Baby Boomers' philosophy) but instead *work to live*. It is this generation, in particular, who are fuelling the rising number of global nomads as they join the international workforce because they are starting with a significantly different mindset.

Generation Y are different – not better or worse, just different. As children of the Baby Boomers, Generation Y are the largest generation to enter the workforce since the Boomers. Just in the USA, this will number some 80 million. They have only been in the workplace for a few years, yet they have gained a reputation for being overconfident, disloyal and fickle. Arguably this may be because they have been misunderstood and mismanaged by employers, who are still managing them in a format of Baby Boomer or Generation X frameworks. Most importantly, they think about and approach work in a different way partly because they were raised differently. Their Baby Boomer parents told them that they were special and capable of anything – and they were supported by the significant wealth creation of their parents. As high potentials they need lots of reassurance and feedback. They had the opportunity of university and post-graduate education (often funded by their parents); they have been sent around the world (again funded or part-funded by their parents), many with a goal of saving some part of the civilization and the planet. This has not only fed a thirst for knowledge and restlessness but also a need to give back time and effort to society as a whole.

Generation Y have grown up with more freedom and choice, economic prosperity (until summer 2008), higher education with ever-changing technology. They have different priorities and expectations. More importantly they are likely to be the most productive generation of all time because they work differently, harness technology and *change* as part of daily life.

The media portray Generation Y as a generation of rule breakers where drugs and alcohol are in excess. Some have said this is a 'sad generation': overindulged, overprotected and overstimulated. This is a group who have grown up in a digital, internet world where immediacy and energy drive a thirst for information. As such they are insatiable, living to excess and pushing to extremes. They are enquiring, challenging, creative and vibrant. They want and expect more than preceding generations.

I have identified five key themes that characterize Generation Y: change, tech savvy, international mindset, social ethics and confidence. Let's look at each in turn, as they provide important clues to understanding the expectations and aspirations of the new global nomads.

Change

Not only have Generation Y grown up with changing times, but the pace of change is seen as an opportunity to grasp. Their time is now. They have the ability to customize everything to their world. They do not need to buy albums or CDs because they can download the tracks they like to create their own playlists on their iPods; they can create their own personal web pages on Facebook; use the internet to create personal travel plans or roam in a virtual, fantasy world. In essence *they choose*. Hence they want to add their own personality and interests to the world of work – they do not want a job for life and do not pretend to do so (the average job tenure is just 16 months!). The pace of change is frenetic – even the world's number-four tennis player Novak Djokovic says he felt old at the age of 21 with the crop of teenagers coming onto the Grand Slam scene. It's not that they are disloyal; they have just grown up with change. Stagnation is boring; they need challenge and experiences.

Tech savvy

'I watch in awe as my children listen effortlessly to ear-bleeding volume on their iPods whilst texting the world, writing dissertations and holding a conversation with me.' Those are the thoughts of one parent.

Multitasking is the norm. According to Forrester's Technographics Benchmark Study, over 90 per cent of this generation in the USA have a computer, download music or videos and own a mobile phone.[2] They do not need to wear watches because they are 24/7 online and their technology performs multiple functions. They have instant access to information and have never known a world without a computer.

It is estimated that Generation Y spend approximately 15 hours a day using digital media or communications.[3]

International and multicultural

Generation Y are the most travelled generation in history. Their parents encouraged it – gap years – and cheap flights fuelled it. Many have visited Thailand, Central and Latin America along with Africa as well as the USA.

In fact, the former are more likely destinations of choice. It is this desire for diversity and adventure that stimulates the generation, rather than the wealth, size and glamour of the Western world. Globalization has made the world a smaller place, so ethnic products, services and music are much more in reach.

With this international focus and multicultural influences, their aspirations drive them to gain as many career-enhancing experiences as possible. They want to present prospective employers with a multitude of real-life experiences rather than a stack of qualifications. They have developed a personal brand: 'Hire me for the energy and personality, not some time-served qualification (I already have a degree, Master's or MBA anyway).'[4]

Social ethics

Generation Y have grown up with climate change, global warming and images of Third World poverty. They feel socially responsible to make the change for their global colleagues. They are connected via music, video and passion. Through the online video stream, they can see the damage created before the corporate spin kicks in. And it's personal – they have experienced more family breakdown than any generation before. Their global networking means that they relate to peers, not elders. They are searching for true integrity and are willing to challenge. Corporate values need to be more than words. They want to see leaders deliver, not only in the workplace but beyond into the immediate community and the world at large.

Companies need to have 'cool values' around the environment and society. They need to be forward thinking and creative. In this climate it is not surprising that Innocent Drinks – a pure smoothie manufacturer – and Cancer Research have become top talent magnets for the elite of the UK's brightest graduates. Generation Y are seeking work with a mission.

Exuberant confidence

Their parents told them they could achieve anything; and they believed us. They had plenty of opportunities to enhance their abilities through extra-curricular activities and the widest range of sports. They are naturally self-assured and goal driven. They are supremely confident, expecting everything to fall into their laps, and hence massively overestimate their own abilities – they think they will make their mark immediately and will progress rapidly in organizations. They are just a click away from the answer! However, the transition from student life to hard graft can be quite a shock. The global recession blew a hole in their expected view of 'entitlement to jobs' – many are struggling to find serious vocational employment 18 months after graduating. But instead of becoming depressed by the situation, Generation Y simply take off with parental funding to seek out new opportunities – teaching English as a foreign language in Vietnam, helping to build new schools in Angola or saving turtles in Costa Rica. This generation think the workplace should adapt to the new (their) world whilst the Baby Boomers and Gen X conformed to meet the corporate norms.

Image

Two other key points to note are that these changes are occurring at an ever-increasing pace, which means generational change may occur within five to 10 years in the future; but importantly, these changes are occurring on a global basis as Generation Y in particular have utilized the internet to forge multicultural community networks transcending national boundaries of geography, distance, language, culture and time zones. This ability to communicate verbally and visually, physically and virtually is the catalyst for the rise of the global nomad.

The management problem is that the Baby Boomers (and Generation X) have not woken up to what happens next. Generation Y are predicted to become the most productive cohort in the modern workplace[5] but they come with attitude. It is time for organizations to wise up as this group are different; they are demanding but at the same time *Absolutely Fabulous*. It is time for international firms to engage.

Now for the first time organizations have four distinct generations employed in the workplace. Generation Y – those born after 1983 – have arrived with some impact. Most organizations have said 'OK, but we are not going to change simply because they have different values,' but this is a sure-fire recipe for disaster as Generation Y will be tomorrow's engine room of your organization.

Before we look in detail at this new professional cadre, it is important to consider the characteristics of the emerging and developing markets.

References

1 www.statistics.gov.uk.cci/nugget.asp?id=170
2 Forrester Technographics Benchmark Survey 2008: 'Gen Y: a generation apart', 039967, 8 August 2008.
3 The Generation Y Survey, www.askgeny.com
4 Ibid
5 Jim Matthewman 'Why CEOs Need to Understand Gen Y'

The emerging and developing markets

03

Many business people and economic commentators casually refer to the emerging and developing markets as if there is a clear and accepted classification that we all can relate to. Yet most people are not exactly sure what these markets are or on what basis their categorizations have been agreed. Indeed, some organizations refer to underdeveloped, emerging, emergent, developing, and Third World markets.

There are no World Trade Organization (WTO) definitions of 'developed' and 'developing' countries. Member countries announce for themselves whether they are developed or developing. However, other members can challenge the decision of a member to make use of provisions available to developing countries. In general, developed countries are considered to be the member countries of the Organisation of Economic Co-operation and Development (OECD) (other than Mexico, the Republic of Korea and Turkey), plus the new European Union member countries that are not OECD members (Bulgaria, Cyprus, Estonia, Latvia, Lithuania, Malta, Romania and Slovenia), plus Israel.

The OECD is a Paris-based club for industrialized countries and the best of the rest. It was formed in 1961. By 2003, its membership had risen to 30 countries, from an original 20.[1] Together, OECD countries produce two-thirds of the world's goods and services. In contrast, 'developing countries' encompass some four-fifths of the world's 6 billion people, many of them in poverty since these countries account for less than one-fifth of total world GDP according to *The Economist*.[2]

If we use this definition of 'developing' and then superimpose a historical timeline, the pace of change and development is staggering. If we take the modern world (ie post Industrial Revolution), the mature countries of old Europe (the UK, France, Germany, Spain, Portugal, the Netherlands, for example) took nearly 300 years to extend and expand their trading routes and spheres of influence (politically and culturally). Others such as the United States, Russia, Australia and Japan built up their modern trading influence over the past 100 years, notably post-World War II.

With more and more countries seeking and gaining independence plus international recognition through the United Nations and participation in the World Trade Organization and the International Monetary Fund, a new wave of trading partners has emerged, notably India, China, Korea, South Africa and the Middle East – all within the past 50 years. See Figures 3.1 and 3.2.

And so to the millennium in 2000, when a new economic map emerged. Countries previously closed to the wider global trading community suddenly became the focus of rapid investment as the mature economies sought out raw materials, energy sources and cheap labour – examples are Thailand, Taiwan, Vietnam, Indonesia in the Far East, Brazil, Argentina, Mexico and Chile in Latin America, Kenya and Angola in Africa, Hungary, Croatia, the Baltics, Ukraine, Turkey in Europe – all within the past 10 years.

Of course, part of this rapid rise has also coincided with technological change. These developments have meant many countries have been able to leapfrog into the 21st century without having to lay down the huge capital investments formerly required by the incremental development of the mature economies. The most obvious examples are the digital world of the internet and mobile telephony, which have opened up communications and business even to the most remote regions of the world.

But with the latest economic crisis brought on by the greed and credit culture of the mature Western world, there has been a further shift. A new set of global values is emerging – more balanced and more people-centric – intrinsically built on trust and depth of relationships. In effect, the past two decades have been dominated by experts who were able to justify arguments through the power of numbers and hard return on investment criteria. This was exemplified by investment banking computer models that automatically signalled buy, hold and sell signals based on real-time market feeds. These models have been shown to be flawed as they failed to take account of the complex independencies which combined to lead to catastrophic collapse; see 'The Terminator Comes to Wall Street' by Joseph Fuller.[3]

Yet when I look at the emerging and developing markets within the tropics, I am struck by the fact that these are, in the main, traditional, trading nations – usually sea-bound – where deals are finalized by human interaction, past record and trustworthiness. In the Arab world, business is still conducted primarily face to face, with emphasis on introductory protocols, understandings and clarifications, agreement and then price negotiation last. Likewise, Chinese business dealings follow strong protocol on meeting etiquette, notably around reciprocal respect of seniority, presentation and points of clarification followed by a period of reflection and decision. A nod simply means that we understand, not that we agree.

FIGURE 3.1 World exports

World export (% share)

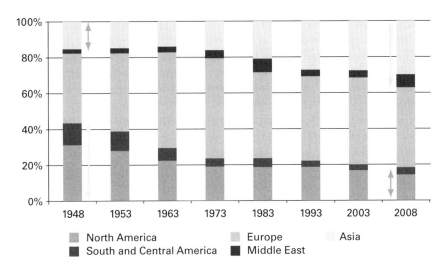

SOURCE: WTO[4]

FIGURE 3.2 World imports

World import (% share)

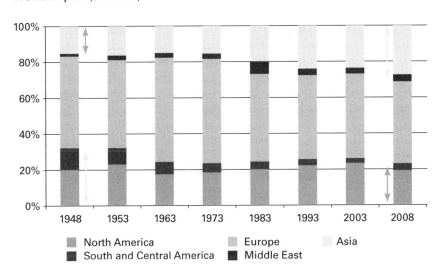

SOURCE: WTO[5]

The second difference with these countries is that their cultures have retained strong inner spiritual and cultural strengths which permeate their organization and business dealings. Arguably this has been lost in the mature markets as Milton Friedman's 1990s market-dominated model of capitalization took hold with Reagan's and Thatcher's endorsement of private sector, profit-driven economics. This hard money, business-first culture was epitomized by Michael Douglas's character Gordon Gekko in the film *Wall Street* with the infamous statement that 'greed, for lack of a better word, is good'. How ironic that Hollywood is preparing a sequel – *Wall Street: Money Never Sleeps* – with much of the original cast.

In contrast Islam, Buddhism, Hinduism and Taoism all put responsibility to wider social community goals as central to their day-to-day actions. Hence personal relationships, integrity and trust form the tripod of business ethics as we look east for future trade. Likewise the dedication to the Catholic Church in some African and Latin American countries would claim a stronger spiritual backbone and commitment to the anomie of many Western countries. In comparison, the underlying tenets of the Eastern religions have strong interlinking similarities.

Growing confidence

Paraphrasing a recent speech by Janet Yellen, the past five years have also seen the emerging countries growing with more political and economic confidence. With each economic cycle they are learning – and arguably at a faster rate than the mature markets. Thus, through the 1980s and 1990s, the Asian tigers (Japan, China, Malaysia, Singapore and the Philippines) were experiencing strong growth and tame inflation, and were encouraged by the international community to liberalize their financial sectors, resulting in a huge influx of foreign capital, typically in the form of short-term loans (capital inflows of $93 billion by 1996). In early 1997 there was a sudden change due to a 'liquidity crisis'; depositors had a loss in confidence with fears of insolvency and doubts over the fundamental soundness of the banks. Whether warranted or not, it became a self-fulfilling prophecy. Consequently there was panic selling as investors tried to unload their holdings of those countries' securities. In addition, there were vulnerabilities in the system due to lack of enforcement of regulations on banks that afforded risky lending practices. This was followed by speculative attacks, claiming the true value of the currencies were misaligned with their pegged values. This led to currency devaluations. Once the pegs collapsed, it led to rapid deterioration of the banks' balance sheets and banks could not service their debt obligations.

Remarkably, a full and fast recovery happened. Between 1999 and 2005, these nations enjoyed average per capita income growth of 8.2 per cent and investment growth averaging nearly 9 per cent, with foreign direct investment booming at an average annual rate of 17.5 per cent. Moreover, all of the loans associated with the International Monetary Fund's assistance programmes during the crisis have been paid back and the terms of those programmes have been fulfilled. At least part of this success was due to policy changes, and increased accounting transparency in the emerging markets has gone some way toward addressing the vulnerabilities. Changing the anchor for these countries' monetary and foreign exchange policies has helped to mitigate the possibility of currency mismatches whilst also allowing for greater domestic flexibility in response to external shocks.[6]

The lessons learned are paying dividends now. Notably there has been a decoupling from the dollar as the sole currency peg; the stock markets of Singapore, Hong Kong and Shanghai are better regulated; there is a better balance of trade and type of trade, which in the past had been largely focused on raw materials, heavy industry and manufacturing (shipping and automobiles and electronics).

Economic growth has also brought political and cultural confidence on the world stage. Communications, notably satellite TV, mobile telephony and the internet, have meant a massive choice of channels and alternative access to information. Former censorships are breaking down rapidly with role models and celebrities not only benchmarked against Western heroes but increasingly in local or regional media. This is stimulating grass-roots development of sport, films, music and art, but the rapid transformation has provided a world platform for these talents. The West is now accustomed to see Eastern star performers such as J Park playing for Manchester United, Yao Ming the Chinese basketball star in the NBA, Liu Xiang (ironically the face of the Beijing Olympics who was unable to compete through injury), plus others such as rock bands, music performers, designers, artists and Indian film stars such as Salman Khan and Sanjay Dutt.

Over the past 10 years, countries like Senegal, Ghana, Nigeria, Ukraine, Turkey, the Republic of Korea, Japan and Australia have all reached the final stages of football's World Cup. Qatar has aspirations to host the World Cup Finals in 2022, having already played host to the 2006 Asian Games and major sporting events on the global tennis, golf and Moto GP circuit. Bahrain, Abu Dhabi, Malaysia, Korea and China now host key Formula One motor-racing events at the expense of Canada and France. The world's richest horse race is the Dubai Classic. The important point here is that examples are not a few but many, plus there is an acceptance both locally and worldwide of the talent: Bollywood is now a serious contender to Hollywood as a key centre of film and showbiz razzmatazz. Likewise the Indian Twenty20 Cricket League is a magnet for major international stars from Britain, Australia, West Indies and South Africa.

This is having a huge impact on the world's younger generations. It is all part of a wider cultural interaction where they are no longer surprised that developing and emerging nations should host and excel at these events. In fact, the events are deliberately used to showcase these nations and encourage tourism as a key economic by-product. These events drive rapid conversion of infrastructure, especially transport but also hotels, convention centres, sports stadia, sanitation and leisure. In the past, major events like these in the mature economies were seen as white elephants – for example, the main Olympic Stadium in Montreal has acquired the nickname 'One-Owe', reflecting taxpayers' anger that it saddled the city with 10 years of debt. But it is not the same in the emerging countries. Major events are major opportunities for change, image and reputation in these nations with their different constructs of ruling families and hence sources of wealth.

Brazil is now seen as the 'New Middle East'. When the notion of the BRIC (Brazil, Russia, India and China) countries was floated, many were surprised at the idea that Brazil was identified as one of the countries to dominate the New World. Its past has been saddled by political unrest, violent crime and shanty-town squalor. Yet over the past 10 years the economic reforms set in motion by Fernando Henrique Cardoso and carried through by President Lula have created a strong growth rate and an economy that was one of the last to be affected by the financial crises and one of the first to come out of recession. Its businesses have been well tested and hardened, yet allowed to be agile and adaptive. Goldman Sachs now predicts that within the next 10 years Brazil will be the world's fifth largest economy.[7] São Paulo is set to be one of the top five cities. This has been born out of its huge natural resources both in minerals and now massive oil finds, but also as major food exporter. It has the fastest-growing middle class in the world, so, unlike its competitors, has both a massive semi-skilled and professional labour force to provide the full range from primary to tertiary industries – from agriculture, mining, manufacturing and engineering to service-based industries. Its companies such as Petrobras, Vale and Embraer are world leaders. Its growth has spurred on new ambition, culminating in it being awarded both the 2014 FIFA World Cup and the first Latin American Olympic Games in 2016.

Political clout

Economic growth has also given a number of the emerging and developing countries geopolitical power. Russia has used its gas supplies to exert renewed political influence over former Eastern Bloc territories, notably Ukraine, but indirectly many of the Central European states. China is now able to negotiate political and economic influence across the Middle East and Africa but is also investing in key material suppliers in the UK (Sinochem buying Emerald Energy) and in Australia (takeover bids for Rio Tinto). The Gulf States, too, have become key investors across the world but notably in UK and US investments.

This economic power has brought increasing weight and influence in the political forum. China has warned the USA not to devalue its substantial investment in US Treasury bonds, whilst Saudi Arabia has won G8 concessions for holding the OPEC cartel in check. Iran and Syria have continued to prompt the USA and the EU to adopt more conciliatory overtures as their regional influence rises.

These moves are prompting greater confidence both as nations but also in terms of individuals' desire and curiosity to reach out across the world. The internet and camera phones mean that images can be beamed instantly across borders into social networking groups or media. This empowerment, particularly of young professionals of both sexes, is driving significant challenge to political regimes across the world, fuelling a sense of global awareness and activism around social causes, whether these be Guantanamo Bay, Iranian elections, Burmese monks, G8 commitments to Africa or humanitarian issues such as Darfur, the Chinese Sichuan earthquake, the Haiti earthquake, the Indian Ocean and Chilean tsunamis, or hurricane or typhoon damage.

The young professionals of today have greater access to information, better understanding of world issues and more confidence in making a statement. Whilst people on the streets and demonstrations remain the prime challenge to unpopular governments, it is the immediacy of the ensuing photos that grabs the world's media. This has meant that in addition to political activism, new environmental causes have also taken centre stage such as HIV, climate change, whaling, commercial logging, toxic waste and famine – all with global coverage. Not only are these issues uniting people across the world but they are notably high on the social agenda of the world's youth as, in their mind, they inherit a planet which has been ruthlessly exploited for profit. Furthermore, as many mature Western economies have weakened over the past 30 years, they are seen to be major perpetrators of environmental abuse as they have had to seek out profit from new sources of raw material or by lax environmental control to maintain existing labour. Examples are the USA's refusal to sign up for the Kyoto Agreement, the UK's willingness to accept nuclear waste from overseas, France's preparedness to test nuclear weapons in Oceania, and Japan's overfishing of whales and tuna. In contrast, some of the emerging countries have capitalized on a growing eco agenda to balance environmental and cultural protection against aggressive commercialization (Costa Rica, Ecuador, Nepal, Kenya, Madagascar and Antarctica). 'Ecotourism' is defined as responsible travel to fragile, pristine and usually protected areas that strives to be low impact and (often) small scale.[8] Ecotourism claims to be a conceptual experience, enriching those who delve into researching. It purports to educate the traveller, provide funds for conservation, directly benefit the economic development and political empowerment of local communities, and foster respect for different cultures and for human rights. Ecotourism appeals to ecologically and socially conscious individuals by focusing on volunteering, personal growth and learning new ways to live on the planet. Once again it is these tenets that appeal most strongly to the new global professional.

Lands of opportunity

The developing and emerging markets have become a prime focus for economic recovery for two reasons. Many provide a source of natural or raw materials which can be converted relatively quickly into economic growth. In the past 25 years, these countries were largely viewed as sources of cheap labour or raw material (mining) to manufacture goods for the mature economies, but exposure of the environmental damage to their environment (the Amazon and Asian rainforests) or exploitation of child labour in the textile industry has prompted both consumer and legislative action to minimize such practice. Now these emerging economies have become magnets for world tourism and higher-value professional services. What this suggests is that economic development of these nations is bypassing much of the industrialization that characterized the mature economies for 50 to 100 years, leapfrogging them into the 21st century's high-growth service sectors, fuelled by a rapidly developing middle-class professional.

Of course, many of these emerging countries (China, India, Vietnam, Brazil and Turkey) have a vast pool of readily available labour willing to move from the fields to the cities. Indeed the rate of urbanization is greatest in these emerging markets.

Furthermore, a feature of these countries is the demographic bias to younger populations. This combination of rural migration and increasing urbanization, available work plus better basic education, has created huge consumer demand not only for products but also for power. This has stimulated a massive shift in trade for some of these nations. Rather than be prime exporters of goods they are now centres for imports, notably fast-moving consumer goods. This in turn part explains why the shift in trade is happening so fast even in some of the poorer nations of the world.

Improving education

The world and the emerging markets recognize that education of the young is a major lever in developing nations. Education – especially reading, writing and mathematics – is the fundamental building block for transforming an emerging market from agricultural dependence to a modern country. Once again, it is the pace of change that is driving the speed of development for many countries. Furthermore, it is the combination of urbanization, education and population growth that is most notable in those emerging countries within the tropics of Cancer and Capricorn.

My hypothesis is that these countries, typically, have a rich history of trading (usually by sea) and hence are more open to other nations, cultures and external influences. Language has always been key to facilitating trade. In the past this might have limited ambitions but the rise of English as the accepted business language of commerce has become a major driver of this growth, along with the rise of a mobile workforce who understand English via education, media and the internet.

References

1 www.oecd.org/document/58/0:3343:en_2649_201185_1889402_1_1_1_1:00. html
2 *The Economist*
3 www.monitor.com/Epertise/CommentariesbyJosephFuller/tabid/173/ctl/ ArticleDetail/mid/887/CID/20081812140322140322152/CTID/1/L/en-US/ Default.aspx
4 *Trade Profiles 2009*, World Trade Organization
5 ibid
6 'The Asian financial crises ten years later: assessing the past and looking to the future', speech to the Asia Society of Southern California by Janet L Yellen, President and CEO, Federal Reserve Bank of San Francisco, 6 February 2007
7 Goldman Sachs
8 en.wikipedia.org/wiki/Ecotourism=cite_note-Honey_EandSD_33-0

PART TWO
The nomads

Introduction

Having set the context, Part Two looks in detail at the new global nomads – their backgrounds, how childhood and university education have shaped their specific professional careers, their distinct behavioural traits, immediate work–life desires and career aspirations. Our 100 global nomads originated from all round the world and whilst half are currently in Dubai and the rest in other international cities as some are already moving on to the next assignment or next phase of life, I have tried to seek out what attracts the nomads to a given city at a given point of their career.

With these insights into their personal motivations, a useful profile appears for those organizations wanting to attract and retain this small but impactful group.

The rise of the professional nomad

04

The drive for new business in the emerging markets has led to a new breed of professional: the global nomads. Manual labour has a tradition of moving to find work all through previous centuries, sometimes of workers' own volition but often by force – slave labour was taken from West Africa to work the cotton fields of Carolina whilst Irish immigrants built the roads and railways of England. In today's world there are still groups of workers who, seeking alternatives to famine and poverty, have migrated to other countries in the hope of finding work: Indian labour is building the new cities of Dubai and Doha; the Poles have taken over much of the UK's hospitality work in hotels, bars and cafes; the Turks are heavily deployed in German manufacturing; Filipino maids are employed throughout the Middle East and Europe. For many of these people, their working life has meant leaving their loved ones behind and a large part of their often meagre earnings being wired home to support extended families. Where large-scale migration occurs, it often produces population concentrations in the host countries to the extent that parts of towns or cities become outposts, such as Brixton or parts of Leeds/Bradford in the UK, the Paris suburb of Clichy-sous-Bois or Slotervaart in Amsterdam. This in turn can lead to difficulties in racial and cultural tensions both in daily life and work. Given the predominant manual focus for most of these people, language typically remains the tongue of their home nation partly for social cohesion and partly due to their level of education. In most cases, however, this working population has moved and settled for a significant period of time in a host country.

What is different today is that world trade is creating professional nomads whose skills are typically concentrated in business communication (advising and negotiation), research and analysis, creativity and design.

These are 'thinking' occupations with a high need to communicate to others in a common format. Computerization has had a major impact here, replacing much traditional hand-written text with screen-based documents complete with inbuilt thesaurus and spellcheckers. In the past 20 years two languages have come to dominate the business world: English and Spanish. East of Cairo, fluency in English is now a mandatory requirement for many professional job applications. The fastest-growing emerging markets are most typically those where historically English has been a second language or where the education system has been sufficiently advanced to ensure the nation's young generation have a sound basis of numeracy and English language. This is why some of the New European countries such as Croatia, Poland, Estonia and Slovakia have outstripped others in economic development, whereas Turkey, and Russia to a degree, are hampered by lower levels of education plus their unique languages. In Asia, India is fast becoming the service centre of the world by being able to latch onto a large young workforce, skilled in both computers and the English language.

Recent recruitment studies by Tata, the huge Indian conglomerate with interests in software and manufacturing, have found a strong relationship between computing and traditional pattern-recognition skills such as carpet weaving and textile. In contrast, whilst China is producing 700,000 engineering graduates per year, only 10 per cent of these can work in multinational companies due to lack of English proficiency and ability to work in a different cultural setting.

Who are these new global nomads?

Individuals in this group often come from families of mixed nationalities in terms of their parents or grandparents. A high proportion were sent to private education in international schools or via emigration to a new school environment in a different country, usually with another language requirement.

> My key memories at school were interests in history and different cultures. I went to an international school with many international friends living all over the world, and had a lot of exposure to tourism, living in New Orleans.
>
> US Generation Y

> I went to an international school, my friends were from all over the place, they were always moving around. I thought I was international but those kids were truly international. I was able to travel a lot around the regions in Asia, with many visits to Bangladesh to visit family. I felt that I had several identities: my Bangladeshi identity, my Filipino identity and then my international identity.
>
> Bangladeshi, Generation Y

I was living in Moscow for elementary school because Dad was a diplomat. I went to a Hungarian school that was attached to the embassy. After four years this closed. My parents decided that I should go to an international school from fifth to eighth grade – it was an international British school. These times were hard, this was when communism had just come to an end and there was a real gap between the richest (tended to be expats and probably the mafia) and the poorest (which was the majority of people). I was ignorant at the time – for me it was natural to have a driver or to order German food from a catalogue – did I really live that life? It was so different from what reality was, expats definitely lived differently from others. All my friends were from all over the world and lived a similar kind of life. I didn't have Russian friends. When we moved back to Budapest it was hard to adjust because I then went to a normal Hungarian school – I really felt different, I couldn't make friends because everything was so different and foreign to what I was used to. I ended up trying lots of different schools... Now I think I'm happy to move around because of experiences I had there and constantly having to adjust. At high school there were definitely two distinct groups, the Hungarians and the internationals and I belonged to the internationals even though I'm Hungarian – I felt more comfortable with the international friends.

Hungarian Generation Y

I was born in Canada. My parents and grandparents were Indian. My memories were always related to international events. I was 10 when the USA attacked Libya. Our American International School in Dubai was surrounded by guards. I was a teenager in Berlin just after the Wall came down but my favourite memories involved exploring new countries and cultures on our family holidays. My father was an oil expat. By the time I went to college I had lived in five different countries and probably visited over 30.

US Generation X

My father was Swedish, my mother Hungarian. Life revolved around school and hobbies such as computers and martial arts – holidays were in northern Sweden with beach holidays in the Mediterranean until my parents divorced.

Swedish Generation X

I was born in Bangkok. My parents were Thai and Taiwanese-Chinese. We made lots of trips back to Thailand and Taiwan so I always wanted to live and work abroad. I remember a school trip to Kyoto. After graduating in Pennsylvania, USA, I worked in London, Hong Kong, Singapore and Sydney.

Thai Generation X

I was born in 1971 in Indonesia. My childhood memories were that I had a very great mathematics teacher in my last year of high school. He always spent 30 minutes at the end of each lesson to talk about philosophy, history and social issues – he introduced us to John Nash's game theory, Sigmund Freud, the birth and role of mathematical science, the Renaissance, origins of civilization and the experts of each culture such as Copernicus and Galileo, plus the Roman, Egyptian, Mayan, Chinese and Indonesian cultures. He opened my eyes and inspired me to see to other sides of the world.

Indonesian Generation X

I grew up in Italy but went to an international boarding school. There was a strong push for international understanding and cultural awareness and we had lots of international students that came from conflicting countries, for instance Israel and Palestine.

Italian Generation X

I am British/Ghanaian with a Dutch mother. My childhood was largely spent in the UK, where I went to cosmopolitan schools that catered for those from colonies, the Commonwealth, and for military families and diplomats.

British Baby Boomer

I've lived in Lebanon, Iraq and the UK. My parents worked for the UN. In 1982, because of the Israeli invasion we moved to Iraq where I was in an international school, where I encountered lots of different nationalities and cultures. Then I moved back to Lebanon, but there was continuous civil war and by 1989 there was another major war, so I moved to the UK and completed my studies in another international school.

Lebanese Generation X

I was born in Algeria, but left when I was three – now I'm curious to go back and see where I was born. Then I spent seven years in Syria for primary school. Then we had five years in Libya and 15 years in the Netherlands – where I finished high school and university. We moved so often to avoid trouble from one country to the next; I never chose to move. It was always a challenge as a kid to start from zero at each new place. It was hard saying goodbye to friends so often, but on the other hand I have always found my way. But then moving to the Netherlands with a new language it felt like I was starting from less than zero – it was a huge step. Living in Europe was very difficult at first, as I found it was offending my culture sometimes. There was also a massive gap in people's knowledge of Arabic countries, so I was constantly having to dispel myths. I think it made me assertive, social and open-minded – but I am still looking for stability, I couldn't really tell you what that is. I don't worry about new challenges, in fact I look forward to them. I've never really known what routine is – I live for the day because I know how bad it can be.

Iraqi/Dutch Generation X

Up to three years I was in Morocco, then Russia, then Australia and back to Russia again. I remember local school in Australia, growing up in an environment and culture that have stayed very deep within me. When I went back to Russia I couldn't say I felt at home there. I am used to living in a slightly different way.

Russian Generation X

My father was the regional manager of an international bank. I was born in Pakistan, then we moved to Abu Dhabi, then Jordan and the UK. All before I was three. I grew up in Nigeria and my early teens were in Cairo. I went to boarding school in the UK. My parents were now in Abu Dhabi at this point and now Dubai. I could never have constant friends.

Pakistani Generation X

They are most typically graduates, and whilst many have additional qualifications such as a Master's or an MBA, they are also likely to have a PADI diving qualification or TEFL (Teaching English as a Foreign Language) certificate. They come with a sense of adventure.

I went to a small college in Southern California to study economics. I did several summer internships in the Philippines. I was also able to visit countries such as Egypt, China, Scotland and Switzerland with the Modern UN Program. Halfway through my degree I joined the military and I was deployed to Kuwait. This opened my eyes to travel, for instance I was able to stop in Spain for a week – it was the first time I was exposed to an international atmosphere, I was like 'Holy crap, there's a whole other world out there' and opened up my mind, which had a profound effect on me. Just to give you some idea of the significance and insight into the majority of Americans, my parents had never left the USA until they came to visit me here in Dubai last year. The USA is so large and diverse that there was never the need to go abroad.

American postgraduate

I went to university in Michigan, then to Wharton for an MBA – I graduated with distinction and learnt 'the American way'. It was a time when Lotus Notes and 123 were issued, Reaganomics and cable TV were launched plus yet another American war. My aim was to return to Venezuela and work in the oil industry. Instead I got a job in Philadelphia and a chance to work in a global environment. I have had five employers in 25 years and still love what I do; still learning every day.

Venezuelan Baby Boomer

I studied mathematics in Indonesia and then a post-graduate in management in the Philippines – my classmates came from such varied backgrounds and their countries. This has helped me deal with people from different countries. This is really important to me. At the time there was huge political change going on; I listened to Queen and lots of R&B.

Indonesian Generation X

I studied biochemistry and management at Imperial College and then a Master's degree. First degrees at university were boring, with tunnel vision and set stereotypes. There were huge events occurring – Mandela being freed and the Berlin Wall coming down. I mixed with similar global travellers and they are still in touch today.

Pakistani Generation X

I studied finance in Boston with a semester in Spain, a semester in Egypt, Germany and Dubai, and spent some summers in Ghana. I loved the travel and meeting so many different people, I loved the people in Ghana. The studying in Egypt was a highlight – I loved the city, the culture – there were so many things to do and see. I took a lot of courses that really fascinated me in Egypt like Arabic, courses in Islam and Middle Eastern history. Ghana was another highlight – I was working in an orphanage for half the time and the other half I was helping with developing long-term sustainability solutions for poverty and helping implement them. I also volunteered in Boston at a homeless children centre.

German Generation Y

I studied business, mathematics and computer science in the Netherlands. It was very international and multicultural – I had more freedom and got a chance to do some travel – I spent some time in Spain, Italy, Tunisia, Syria, Egypt, Turkey, Lebanon, Jordan, France, Germany, Belgium, UK.

Iraqi/Dutch social scientist

In April 2003 my boyfriend and I took three years off to travel through central Asia, New Zealand, Africa, Eastern Europe, South and Latin America. The highlights were Antarctica and Galapagos, my husband proposing in the Cook Islands, our wedding in the Czech Republic, attending the Olympics in Athens, seeing white sharks and mantra rays in Mozambique, tracking rhinos in South Africa, mountain gorillas in Uganda, visiting Petra in Jordan, and snowboarding in Idaho. Now with four-year-old twins we travel to close locations like Singapore.

Thai Generation X

We sisters were born in Melbourne of mixed nationality – Australian and Filipino. I always wanted to leave home – went through an American and then an Asian phase. I remember my dad telling me about his time travelling with the navy.

Australian Generation X

They are usually aged between 23 and 35 – thus mainly Generation Y and Generation X. They will normally have had some work experience in their native country before having made the decision to pack up to seek employment elsewhere. Money is less of a driver for seeking out these new careers but more importantly this group are basically 'up for challenge'. They are sometimes disillusioned with home-grown native politics, drudgery of daily commuting or stifling attitudes, especially towards different races or religions.

My first serious job was in engineering in Los Angeles. My career expectations were unclear and more driven by experience (lifestyle, social, travel, career). The secondary driver was money. I moved because I wanted to get away from the USA/Canada. I wasn't so concerned about what the job was. At the time my key memories were being broke, using a cellphone. My favourite song was 'Working for the Weekend'. I remember walking on the beach and being in Hollywood.

British-Canadian Generation X

Career advancement is important for me. I had expected that the company would take care of me and its staff, this was a more important factor than the money. But I remember the feeling of being at the bottom of the ladder, relearning the rules, felt like starting school again. I have always been interested in technology and this meant I was able to keep in touch with people all over the world easily.

Filipino Generation Y

Career development was very important to me and being in an environment that I felt I could see myself in five years' time with room to grow. I wanted to be doing things that challenged and stretched me. I also wanted it to be diverse in terms of work and work colleagues.

Indian Generation X

My first job was as an IT analyst for Morgan Stanley in London and Hong Kong. My memories were of the handover of Hong Kong, Lady Diana's funeral and a Nokia mobile that was the size of a banana. I have had five employers in 13 years.

Thai Generation X

I was one of the Thatcher generation, working in London at the time of the Balcombe Street siege and Band Aid. My first proper car was an Alfa Romeo; I had money to dress fashionably, listening to 80s electronic music by Ultravox with an aim to be an occupational psychologist. My first job on leaving the UK was in France, then South Africa (girlfriend was Finnish; first wife South African; second partner French). Moved around a lot every two or three years; co-founded a firm, then moved out to Asia into a series of regional roles covering Japan, Korea, China, Hong Kong, Taiwan, Philippines, Thailand, Brunei, Indonesia and Australia.

English Baby Boomer

I got a job with Emirates airline which brought me to Dubai – I had little expectations as I had just realized where it was on the map. I was 21, my first time to really party and go out. I had my dream job, the one my career counsellor said was virtually impossible – never thought that I would get sick of it and want to leave. I have now worked for five companies usually for about two to three years.

Australian Generation Y

I went to university in Chennai to study engineering but as a day scholar it was very studious with virtually no time spent on leisure. At the age of 23 my first job was for an IT firm in India. My key memory of this time was the first cricket World Cup held in India. My career expectation was to have steady growth and the opportunity to travel to different countries – I had lived in India for 23 years! I worked for three firms before I decided that I needed to work for a multinational firm.

Indian Generation X

I had lots of high expectations. I'm an ambitious person and I like challenges. Didn't find the internship challenging enough, I wanted an international career, I wanted a steep learning curve and lots of development.

Irish Generation Y

I loved my first serious job in London; went out a lot, dated loads. I moved from finance to consulting and then retail. I did not really like the numerical approach where I was living in spreadsheets all day. I preferred working more on relationships and wanted more creative work so when the job came up at Nike, I jumped at it.

Swedish Generation X

I graduated as a chemical engineer, had a Vauxhall Nova but wanted any two-seater soft-top sports car. Loved all the 80s bands, Duran Duran, Spandau Ballet, Frankie Goes to Hollywood – I had huge permed hair! I stayed with ICI for 20 years but took three breaks; one was an MBA which was very multicultural. Moved to Shanghai with the company – my husband followed. I became a freelance HR consultant, then a role reversal when I followed my husband (oil man) to Dubai; took a break and resurrected my freelance HR career.

British late Generation X

They are seeking out a promise of challenging work balanced with an energetic active lifestyle of like-minded folk. They are incredibly social; living alone in a new city such as Dubai is not an issue as at one level as within weeks there will be work and social networks that create groups keen to interact through sports, eating and drinking, arts and other leisure choices. But as these responses show, the emotional ties run deep.

Why Dubai? Because I had never been and I had heard it was full of talented people from all over the world (I guess I missed that environment).

Working with and getting to know people from all over the world. The Islamic culture and their view on life. I find it amazing and fascinating, when you really think about it, that people from all over the world, from such different backgrounds and experiences are able to understand and work with one another. However, I do miss family, boyfriend and everyone who is close to me back home.

After university in Stockholm, I immediately left for London as I wanted to become an investment banker and London was where the jobs were. It was 2000, full of IT hype and the millennium, soaring stock prices. I resigned from Morgan Stanley to join a hedge fund but was fired after eight weeks. I then joined another investment bank but was made redundant at the start of the financial crisis. I had four employers with an average tenure of about 19 months. I am now back in Sweden enjoying a consulting role in retail real estate.

Some people complain about the lack of culture but that's not true. It is only a matter of going out to find out about the events. The key is to explore. There are now a few thousand Twitters and since joining I have never been more up to date with what is going on. Twitter works great in a small city for networking and keeping others informed.

I like that Dubai is so centrally located and close to Europe and Asia. I like that I can go on a weekend trip to visit my parents in India. It's such a diverse place – you don't feel like you are living in the Middle East. It's a good balance between working hard and an easy life – I wouldn't call New York an easy life. Even though Dubai pretends to have this mask of modernity, underneath it all it's still developing, it's not like Europe, nothing here is structured and it takes a long time to get things done. I like that here you aren't expected to pretend to be someone and fit into a certain culture – you can be different from anyone else and still be accepted. But I miss India – I miss the warmth of the people and their hospitality, I miss the food and the laid-back lifestyle and of course my family.

I really wanted to work in a cosmopolitan city and because of my background I wanted to be in the Middle East. Dubai was the most open and developed place. I really like being in an international environment, in a booming city with plenty of opportunities and a place where I feel I can learn. The sun was also a massive attraction, I like to see the sun and the beach every day, and it makes me feel more optimistic each day.

Working outside Indonesia in the 90s was a big move for me – it was very difficult at that time especially to go to the States because you needed to have graduated from US universities or other 'notable' countries. I move around a bit – first Canada, then the US, Philippines and now Singapore. I love my current role as I can explore other emerging markets that are quite new to me. I like the challenge and the opportunities to learn.

I love the fact that I can travel a lot and meet people from all over the world, it's easy to make friends here. I like that everyone is different, so you aren't treated as an outcast or a foreigner here. I like living without tax, it means that we can live a standard of life that we couldn't live otherwise. Everyone here seems to want to go out and enjoy their lifestyle. Of course, there's the beach and shopping too. I miss walking – everything here has to be done by taxi or car. I don't like how the structure of Dubai is all centred around the highway.

It's more related to the job for me, the diversity of the jobs and countries – I like the variety. It's a different country with a different way of doing things and you adapt to it – it's different being an expat here from being an expat in places like Mozambique. I miss my friends and the beach in Mauritius. However, you don't want to get on the wrong side of administration. Also, I've never felt conscious about my skin colour until I came here.

Dubai was a region that was growing and developing and a place to get on-the-ground experience and plenty of opportunities. Here you get noticed a lot quicker and I thought it would be good for my career. It was also the thrill and excitement of moving to a new place. What I have noticed is that because of the weather, there's a holiday feel about the place, especially at the weekends. It's a young population. Everyone is friendly and good humoured.

Whilst this rapidly growing group is now filled with a kaleidoscope of many nationalities (Mercer's office in Dubai numbers 60 people from 29 different countries), there are a few which trail-blazed the notion and helped pioneer the concept.

The nomads are most widely populated by Australians, New Zealanders, Canadians, South Africans, Nordic, Dutch, Lebanese, Indians, Pakistanis, Aseans, plus Generation Y folk travellers plus those from the USA, UK and Italy. Most recently the nomads have been swollen by many New European and Latin American nationalities – Poles, Croatians, Serbians, Turks, Israelis, Brazilians and Argentinians.

The first group, eg Canadians, Dutch and Scandinavians, emanate from distant shores where younger people find the pace of life at home too pedestrian, narrow and offering few opportunities, yet their societies are very open to liberalism, multiculturalism and open-air pursuits, acting as centres for refugees and sponsors of international diplomacy. The New Zealanders, Aussies and South Africans have histories of internationalism, travel and the extreme outdoor life.

The second group – Indians, Pakistanis and Aseans – have long been migrants seeking out a better life abroad through new work to fund extended families at home. Whilst many of their compatriots have often been the core manual workforce serving the ambitions of their richer employers; their professional middle classes are often the backbone of nascent companies looking to expand and grow internationally. Here their knowledge of accounting, medicine, English and middle (people) management gained through above-average education in their homeland stands them well in the emerging world.

They also display a remarkable capacity to remain ambitious to a given limit, unlike some US or UK counterparts who expect top executive roles, to dominate the middle and senior management positions; knowing that locals may be appointed to the highest positions (not open to them) but who will then be totally reliant and dependant on their professional advice. In the main there is a sense that these guys primarily move for money.

Of most interest is a growing talent flow of young, middle-class, educated professionals from Brazil and Argentina to Europe but beginning to branch out to Asia. These are engineers, young managers, analysts and economists who combine language skills of Portuguese and Spanish plus English with technical and business analysis.

Which leads us to the new 'emerging group' of nomads. These are the exiles of modern wars: a new intelligentsia escaping from the scars of civil wars and political unrest for a different world where order is more predictable, where their skills are valued and they are treated as equals whether they be Muslims, Christians, Taoists, Hindus or Buddhists. To this extent the Lebanese probably lead the stakes as the most nomadic 21st-century population, closely followed by the Palestinians, the Generation Y of Croatia, Serbia, Israel and Iraq. For many in this group, Western democracy has failed to deliver and some of the emerging markets provide opportunity amidst benign one-party or one-ruler states. A key difference of these nomads is that the decision is one of political safety and as such they have left their homeland as families to form communities in another land. Furthermore, as nomads they do not need to actively participate in the local politics as they are simply passing through. For them there are greater wider issues of geopolitics, climate change, environmental damage and alleviation of poverty.

I was born in a Jordanian refugee camp in 1977 as Jordan was the first to offer shelter after the Israeli war of 1967. My parents were both Palestinian who had met in Cairo. My father then got a job as an engineer in Kuwait at the time of the oil rush. Whole communities moved to Kuwait, which became the 'land of opportunity' where

Middle Eastern professionals (engineers, doctors, financiers) were accepted because of their qualifications and it was Arabic speaking. I started school in a private English school but was then transferred to a local public school to give a better grounding in Arabic studies. In 1988 the family moved to Canada – another country which has generously offered shelter and education to displaced communities. My aunt had moved there and so my father and subsequently another uncle followed; in fact, seven related families followed. The decision was purely to enhance the education of myself and my two brothers and sisters. We were treated as equal and had more freedom of speech. Following schooling I attended college in the same city; it meant I could live at home. I studied actuarial science, bought a car – a Honda Accord coupé – and got married to another expat Palestinian. Whilst Canada was a 'Robin Hood' society, I still felt that I was in a minority being a Middle Eastern Muslim where customs were misunderstood. Her family had chosen Dubai as their land of opportunity, so this was a natural first choice for a professional move.

We have no homeland, no base to return to. It was easy to assimilate into Dubai – we had family here (my brother has now joined us and most of our Palestinian friends have extended families here). I now have a young son, we are proud to tell him that he is Palestinian with a Canadian passport and resident in Dubai. We have more exposure to Islam, Arabic channels on TV, a chance to speak Arabic both within and without the family. It is liberal enough and provides great opportunities for travel. Unlike other expats we are well settled here and will want to stay for the foreseeable future. I want to explore more countries, have more solid roots and would probably look to retire in Canada – I am a citizen and we have family there.

Fourth, an interesting group – the rejuvenated oldies. Organizations are finding value in a group of 50-plus-year-olds who as they come to the end of their career have managed to see their young brood into university and into the world of employment and are now released to do the things they desperately wanted to do when they were 25 or 30. This group were denied gap years by their parents. In my case a four-year course in economics and marketing was deemed to be out of the question, let alone any idea of a part-funded 'gap year'.

This group of Baby Boomers have relatively financial security often with home in place in their host country but now have been given or have sought out the opportunity of some final challenges in their world of employment. Given the high number of young nomads in the emerging markets and relative lack of local leaders, this group are perfect for multinational firms to place as old sages for two reasons. One, they can help temper some of the ebullient enthusiasm of so many hot bloods rushing around customers and clients but, secondly, many of the local companies and organizations in such markets desire or indeed require sufficient grey hair in their commercial partners before business can be secured.

> I had been working in Melbourne and wanted a change – a management job came up in Sydney but after two years I then returned but there was a vacuum. I was bored, then a chance came up to do some project work in Singapore. This was an exciting change – a bigger sandpit to play in and with different toys. Whilst I was separated from my wife and family, the opportunities were so huge. We were pioneering new territories. At 48 I felt this was my last big shot. I travelled throughout Asia and home was Singapore Airlines. I realized that I needed different behaviour and a different tone of voice in each country: in Japan you need to speak softly; in China it is much louder; and in India you let them to the talking. One of the by-products is that the family travelled to the most exotic places – they have the bug now.
>
> Australian Baby Boomer, entrepreneur

At a time when there has been so much focus on the younger talent with the danger that a whole generation of post-45-year-olds are thrown on the scrap heap, more and more organizations are beginning to see real value in deploying this group as nomads, albeit for a shorter period – three to five years. Furthermore, these organizations are reporting remarkable, outstanding performance from these individuals as they draw second wind.

> In my 20s I had yearned for a gap year or the opportunity to go to Australia and New Zealand. Instead I travelled around Europe – Greece, Italy, Holland, Denmark and Germany. With a good income in my late 20s, suddenly I had the opportunity to travel to the Far East with my girlfriend. Twenty-plus years on, our children – son and daughter – are now Generation Y adults who asked for gap years. We have become gap-year parents following the course of these wonderful free spirits. Our deal was simple – you earn and we will match your earnings to create the fund and we shall meet halfway in time wherever that might be. It turned out to be Mexico/Costa Rica for my daughter and French Polynesia for my son. Now in later years I can feel the vibrancy of the new kids on the block and can help mentor both in technical and business transactions.
>
> UK Baby Boomer

Well travelled and multilingual

Awareness through news coverage and curiosity through documentary TV programmes plus the availability of air travel has meant today's generations are more travelled than ever before. Unlike previous generations, the number of people who have travelled or worked in more than 10 countries certainly outnumbers their relative number of employers.

Travelling isn't as big an objective as it was before because I get to travel so much with work. I go home whenever I want – there is no set rule for this, just go when I feel like it – travelling by plane has become so natural to me that it doesn't feel any different from taking a train to the next city – the world is a village, you can move from one country to another.

Singapore is the 12th city in the seventh country in four continents that I have lived in in 25 years. I speak five and a half languages (just a little Chinese) and have travelled to over 65 countries in all the continents. I have worked in 36 countries in all the continents except for Antarctica, so I think I am pretty nomadic!

I have consulted to more than 2,500 organizations in over 35 countries in the past 27 years; every assignment, every day is an adventure to explore cultural diversity – and there are many more to come.

But when this is analysed by age, the number of countries visited by individuals aged under 30 is growing exponentially. In addition to travel, the number of people who can speak two or more languages fluently has also grown substantially. In the past 10 years, more and more European, Middle Eastern and Asian Generation X and Generation Y have learned English at school in addition to their native tongue. The overwhelming, almost overbearing, availability of Western movies, TV shows and music has also meant that English has become the dominant language of the new generations. So much so, larger local and international organizations have adopted English as either their main or second business language. It is virtually a requirement for all senior managers and executives to be fluent in English, even where states have adopted aggressive nationalization quotas.

The use of more or less standard qwerty keyboards for computers and mobile phones has reinforced the use of English as the prime language for both business and social communication. And this will only increase.

The impact of the growing use of English is twofold. First, it has made leisure travel for Generation X and Generation Y far easier – in fact, it is far more likely that when travellers visit far-flung destinations of the world where they might be keen to practise their newly learned phrases in Spanish, French, Chinese, etc, the opposite occurs with their hosts keener to practice their English irrespective of where the visitors have originated. English has become the travellers' language.

Second has been the impact in the United States and the UK. The growing use of English as the world's travellers' and business language has created a growing laziness to learn other languages. Hence the proportion of individuals aged over 45 who are fluent in another language in these countries is lower whilst amongst their Generation Y and Generation X group the number of students taking degrees in a foreign language or as a subsidiary major is rising rapidly.

All of which means the global nomads are not only well qualified, they are also well travelled and multilingual. Being multilingual is a huge asset in the emerging markets because even though a nomadic professional might not be able to speak the local language or a given dialect, their awareness of the importance of language provides them with the fundamentals of multicultural understanding.

Of the 100 global nomads I interviewed around the world, 75 had at least three languages and 10 per cent had four or more. Everyone had fluency in English but a growing number also had Spanish or Portuguese. A third were currently studying a new language either relevant to their current location, eg Arabic or Mandarin, or have set their sight on another future location.

This higher awareness of difference ensures a patience, respect and acceptance of a different way of doing things. Thus, verbally and visually, the nomad is better able to read and sense the mood of a meeting, unlike the 'fly-out' expats who try to dominate conversations and meeting agendas with huge doses of patronization. Furthermore, as we all know, simple translation of words into the local language is rarely enough as the idioms and syntax will be different. The need for local language in business is important in two respects – one with the highest-level decision makers but also when implementation and execution are required, as a large proportion of the 'doers' may be locals without English fluency.

The new global nomad is far more likely to listen first, seek clarification and understanding before launching into some form of Western-style agendas and force decisions in meetings. The latter does not work in the Middle East, China or other Asian markets. In emerging markets, the customer or client will set the tempo, mood and objectives. These meetings are more about getting to know you first before discussing any business opportunities or agreeing terms of business. Both socially and in business there are clear protocols to be observed and respected.

It would seem from my 100-nomad sample that a high proportion have been brought up in families with mixed nationalities, which again has prompted both greater travel as they were growing up and multiple fluency.

Previously, expats sent abroad in the 1970s to 1990s sought out their own exile communities complete with exile clubs – even creating their own country communities within their new homeland. Thus Singapore has its four quadrants for Arabic, Indian, Chinese and Malay, Hong Kong has its St Andrew's Society and Calcutta Club, San Francisco has its famed Chinatown and Little Italy, London has Little Venice and, for Australians, Earls Court, Melbourne has its Greek area (home to the second-largest Greek population outside Greece), New York has its Italian sector, and Sydney has its Little Hanoi.

But in the new modern cities of Doha, Dubai and São Paulo, the opposite applies whereby the global nomads are by definition less interested in their own cultural heritage and national backgrounds but more in those of others.

I have been an expat for a number of years in different cities but when I came to Dubai, my husband and I made a conscious effort to shun my home-landers and seek out new relationships from other countries.

Dutch Generation X in a multinational logistics firm

I had always wanted to have the experience of living and working overseas but my husband less so. When I was offered Shanghai, he felt he could easily further his career there and our children were young and portable. If we did not take this chance, we might not get another. When I finished my posting the company expected that I would return to the UK but we had enjoyed overseas living so much that we both started new jobs in the Middle East and Asia. We did not specifically choose Dubai but as an expat it is a very easy place to live and work compared with Shanghai – the language and cultural barriers are significantly lower.

British Generation X HR director

Partly due to the circumstances of individuals meeting in a third land and partly though the intrigue of seeking out new friendships, any relationships formed will often focus on at least two or more languages. For those who form lasting relationships and create their own families, there is a high probability of their offspring becoming multilingual. These young offspring can have a fascinating mix of blood.

We have two children under seven, we speak German and Danish to them and they learn English and Arabic at school.

German and Danish expats

But here is an interesting paradox between nomads who have left their homeland of birth often out of disillusionment, yet once in a relationship or with a family, there are a few heart strings to share. The question is how strong are these pulls and at what point does the nomad return (if at all).

It's not my first time out as an expat. It's a good opportunity to visit new places, new cultures, and experience the freedom. But there is a flip side of the coin – whilst you are young you can travel, but there's a certain time when you need to have a place to come back to and call home. You can't travel your whole life – but I am still searching for the country that I shall call home.

I find myself feeling frustrated when I return to Europe by the little change in the way things work, things I didn't like are still the same. And because I've worked in such dynamic environments, I guess I find myself wondering why things here don't change so quickly.

I find it amazing and fascinating, when you really think about it, that people from all over the world, from such different backgrounds and experiences, are able to understand and work with one another. But I miss my family, boyfriend and everyone who is close to me back home.

We decided that we would only go home just once a year and we would use our holidays to explore the regions we were living in. When we go back to the UK, we realize how obsessed the British are with their houses and gardens!

I usually go back to England about four times a year, these are usually fairly short visits. I miss the greenery but I note that people tend to have a rather grey, down and pinched expression. Everybody seems to dress in the same in dull colours.

It's wetter in Ireland! It's seems like it rains more than it ever did. You notice that nothing ever changes – the same people are still doing the same things and going to the same places.

The term homeland is confusing for me – is it Palestine, Kuwait or Jordan? When I have gone back I do not feel much changed in Jordan since I left 10 years ago.

My husband travels a lot, so sometimes it is nice just to not be travelling. I'd like to travel around Asia and the Indian Ocean. I prefer active holidays and sightseeing – but there needs to be a balance, especially with a baby. Most of our holidays are back home, once every three months on average. Time is never enough, it's very difficult to organize, and especially in Istanbul the distances are very long. I miss it a lot.

I like to take short vacations doing something active like hiking. I take two types of vacations – for fun and for going back home to see family. I go back twice a year. Going back you see people are continuously changing, relatives are growing up. The country hasn't really changed. You feel there is a gap between you and your previous life.

An energetic, can-do mentality

A key feature of this new band of professionals is their attitude. Unlike some criticism of today's young, it comes with strong purpose. There is an overall sense of 'can do' and 'let us get on with it'. Sure, they are happy to be briefed, given a clear sense of direction – but not micro-managed. Once the task is delegated to them, they expect that the responsibility lies with them as individuals and as a team. They are also quite content to have check backs, milestone reporting, but for them achieving the end goal is the priority. They like personal briefings, manager and *peer* feedback on a less formal one-to-one basis. This is a group that have always sought out confirmation and acceptance from their parents, rather than confrontation and rebellion.

These new younger nomads are up for challenge; the bolder, more inventive, creative and innovative the better. These individuals are more likely to choose an outdoor, extreme sporting holiday than a known resort beach hotel. This thirst for knowledge, adventure and most of all new experiences is the prime driver.

Their favourite books are likely to be a mixture of classics (eg Tolstoy's *War and Peace* or Sun Tzu's *The Art of War*), cultural exposés or alternative viewpoints on economics or the wider universe, such as *Freakonomics*, *Girls in Riyadh*, *India's Unending Journey*, *Berlin: the Downfall* or some different exploratory travel guide, eg *Trekking in Oman* or *Fifty Places to Dive before You Die*. Most interestingly, one book stands out well above others for this group (30 per cent of nominations): *The Kite Runner* by Khaled Hosseini.

For these people, staff meetings without clear purpose, general talking shops, decision-making processes requiring committee papers, consensus voting and numerous versions before clearance are anathema. Use of time is very important for individuals who have grown up multitasking. Their day is too short as, in their universe, their attention span for corporate bureaucracy is simply satisfying outdated, reporting lines. For this group information flow is primarily a single, horizontal plane gushing upwards and sideways and less about top-down or bottom-up processes.

In essence the nomads are confident, very result orientated, thrive in groups – ever-changing teams rather than a set team – they want to do well and be recognized for their effort and want to be seen to do the 'right thing'.

Strong social priorities

The nomads are highly social: even though some may be relatively shy, their use of mobile phones and social networking sites allows a much higher degree of connectivity than pure one-to-one, face-to-face interaction. It also means they have greater control over where and when to pick these interactions, allowing some to keep work and leisure very separate and private whilst for others the world of work and their social life become completely blurred. Witness the recent 'flash raves' where people simultaneously converge on Liverpool Street Station to either protest or create a 'gathering'. Terminology is also changing around text-based slang parties: parents are similarly 'rents' (nice irony here!), parties are now called 'gatherings', implying a looser invitation list, 'atm' which means 'at the moment' or 'lol' which means 'laugh out loud' or 'great' abbreviated to 'gr8'.

This high degree of choice is fundamental for the nomad and it means corporate cultures, rules and protocol have less impact and less relevance. In fact, the nomads have a much higher regard for individual respect and tolerance.

Besides their ability to bring relatively large numbers of like-minded folk together physically or virtually, they also, in the main, share a strong sense of social consciousness. The support for sporting or leisure events is likely to be greater and have higher commitment if the cause is seen as worthwhile and there is a genuine chance that time, money and sweat will see donations channelled to needy causes. These causes are less likely to be politically constructed and more likely from passionate real-life cases where the organizer has had direct first-hand contact with the particular cause, whether this is motor neurone disease, poverty or education in Africa or volunteering in Central America.

The nomads' desire to see as much of the world as possible has stimulated a huge respect for the natural environment, cultural diversity, awareness of the huge disparity in terms of the poor, starving and mistreated and those in richer societies. However, the drive to save the planet from political and corporate excess is not so much from rallying around some coordinated revolutionary challenge – these, of course, exist – but more from a personal commitment to make a difference: a willingness to set aside some private quality time or to join others in a volunteering trip that has an end goal. There is a strong sense that the nomads like the idea of having active fun and doing good at the same time. The Band Aid concert in 1985 set this off in the mid 1980s but now there is a whole spate of events, locally, regionally and globally, such as Live8 and tsunami relief.

Transferable skills – and where next?

05

The new nomads have grown up in a world of computers, internet, connectivity through digital media, TV spotlights, satellites and instant messaging. They have information at their fingertips – literally. These computer-savvy individuals are highly numerate (a very high proportion of them state that mathematics or economics were their favourite subjects at school – nearly twice the second-favourite category of English or another language). See Table 5.1.

They also benefited from a significant curriculum change; for example, in the UK the many school subjects in the 1970s and 1980s saw a shift from the rote learning of the 1960s to greater interpretation of concepts and application to specific situations. University education also changed to reflect a strong bias to case study references. This means the new global nomads come ready primed.

They are highly numerate, very analytical, structured in approach, diligent in process methodologies and focused on outcomes.

They fall into two groups – those which have broad business know-how or deep technical skills. A high proportion have business-related degrees in economics, international business, business administration, which can be applied in internal or external advisory or consulting roles, or strong customer-facing skills such as sales, marketing or public relations. These skills lend themselves to high revenue-generating initiatives that are typically cyclical in nature in both in terms of commercial opportunity and location, prompting both employer and employee movement to seek out the next 'wave' of opportunity. This is perpetuating the nomadic lifestyle.

TABLE 5.1 Favourite school subjects

Order	Favourite school subject
1	Mathematics
2	Sciences
3	Economics / Business
4	Languages
5	History
6	Geography
7	Humanities
8	Social Sciences
9	Literature
10	Arts

SOURCE: 100 global nomads interviewed by Jim and Miles Matthewman, 2010[1]

My key skills are interpersonal skills, structural thinking (ie able to organize and put pieces of puzzle together), analytical, presentation skills, quick learner, entrepreneurial and open to challenges.

Given I started out on a fast-track management programme, I had expectations that I would be promoted twice within a five-year period but my most notable job change was after completing my MBA. This was a great way to switch careers. I have the opportunity to work across geographies and interact at the highest levels in client organizations. My key skills include flexibility, innovation, ability to complete projects in a timely and efficient manner plus highly developed interpersonal skills.

I can adapt to different environments, I feel that I fit in easily because I understand that there are cultural differences and I am open to this.

My key skill is that I am quick in understanding, I can put pieces together and then draw from multiple sources.

Relationship skills by far number one; especially in an environment where it is more informal, young, vibrant and sports orientated.

I feel challenged every day and am still learning. The moment that I don't feel challenged I will leave. The challenges have been aligned with my goal of 29 and a half – nothing to do with money but moving up in the company.

My key skill is that clients like me. They feel that I have their interests at heart and will do whatever it takes to help them.

I am organized, multitask well, technically savvy and love project-based work anywhere within the business.

I'm detail orientated, I'm quick at solving problems and client-centric.

My skills are interpersonal skills and cultural sensitivity, managing relationships and establishing credibility. I believe I have the ability to make things happen and implementation of ideas. A strength is creative thinking; connecting the dots and proposing ideas.

My key skill is to think differently and bring more than one perspective to bear on a topic. I work well with others and forge compromises.

The remainder have specialized, operational roles such as engineering, geology, chemistry, physics or project management. The latter, of course, are by definition project based, moving from one location to another, delivering outcomes which typically have medium-term time frames from six months to three years. When a given assignment finishes, their employer looks for the next opportunity to utilize these high-value skills.

This is, of course, extremely convenient for the multinational employer providing flexibility of deployment on the grounds of business need but it has a downside, to the advantage of the employee. Unlike previous generations where the majority of Western business was centred around technical expertise, notably for manufacturing, in today's service-based economy these skills are highly transferable. The skills are more knowledge based with less employer control on intellectual ownership or property. Customers and clients are buying the individual as much as the content, experience and reputation of the employer. In this context the individual has become more of a free agent with a much higher degree of choice in deciding to stay with a given employer or moving from one to another.

Given the new professional nomads' propensity to seek out new experiences, new locations and new challenges, loyalty is no longer to a given employer (as typified by tenure of Baby Boomers) or to a given profession (as with Generation X), but now is more diversified and blurred. The attraction of the nomads to employers is more around their broad portfolio of commercial skills, their experience of different business cultures, their language capability, interpersonal skills (both in terms of leadership and external relationship building) plus vibrant energy. These personal attributes give the nomads significant negotiating power. And they know it.

What are the underlying drives of the nomad?

The nomads have an insatiable desire for new experiences and thirst for knowledge. Their sense of personal destiny means that they feel empowered to take rapid decisions – there is little procrastination: if opportunities present themselves they can quickly pack up and go. This mirrors the many leisure opportunities they experience. The era of cheap air travel and internet connectivity means that events or 'gatherings' can be pretty spontaneous, irrespective of where they are taking place. This is part of the challenge. And so is the nomads' attitude to future work careers.

Playing to Generation X and Generation Y strengths

The post-Lehman world plays to the relative strengths of the Generation X and Generation Y professionals. The new world order, reflected by the extension of the G8 to G20 and BRIC/BIIC (Brazil, India, Indonesia, China) country demands to the International Monetary Fund (IMF),[2] combines a much wider perspective than the prior predominately Western European interests. These additional countries are experiencing rapid growth in new industries and technology. Their starting point is different, the old orthodoxy is less relevant and there is a willingness to consider and experiment with new ideas. In fact, given that the old orthodoxy has failed, there is great pressure to find what is being termed 'the new normal' as coined by Mohamed El-Erian, CEO of PIMCO, the world's largest bond investor. He predicted long-term growth in the mature markets will be depressed by consumer retrenchment and rising financial regulation.[3]

The global nomads are already searching for this open-minded adventure. Part of leaving the homeland was frustration with the stagnation and tinkering of old-school established management theory of the mature countries' workplace. The emerging markets offer variety, breadth and a chance to personally shape new solutions and put new workplace theories and practice into place. These markets allow the professional the freedom to experiment in both physical and intellectual space.

The skylines of Dubai, Abu Dhabi, Doha, Singapore, São Paulo and Shanghai are testimony to this innovation – an architect's and engineer's paradise to indulge in fantasy projects such as the Burj Khalifa, Palm Jumeriah, Yas Island, The Pearl, Scott's Tower, The Oriental Pearl Tower or Ponte Estaiada in São Paulo.

Yet in the mature markets, projects are often amendments, revisions or conversions of existing practice and thereby more limiting in scope or constrained by budgetary or regulatory parameters. In the emerging markets, plans tend to be greenfield, novel, grand, with less restriction in design or financial control, offering the professional the chance to realize start-to-finish completion, thereby providing a much higher sense of fulfilment and achievement.

But here is the reality. The US and European construction giants (Bechtel, Arup, Laing O'Rourke, Balfour Beatty) have been cautious in their overseas expansions – wanting to keep subsidiary offices 'in Europe with a few outposts in English-speaking cities', ie South Africa, Dubai, Hong Kong and Sydney. But as Figure 5.1 and Table 5.2 show, the work forecasted in the next five years will be in very new emerging markets. Morocco has already set down its marker to build the next tallest building in the world.

Many of these construction companies are now seeing that much of their revenues are coming from the Middle East, Australia (less impacted by the recession) and the Far East. In Europe, there has been retrenchment with cost-base reductions; in the Middle East the market collapsed but is recovering through Abu Dhabi, Qatar and Saudi Arabia and the Far East which saw some reduction but remained 'active'. For these construction firms the recession meant a switch in business from a growth private sector market to greater focus on public sector infrastructure projects, notably transport, heath and education projects, many of them in emerging markets. The companies responded by major restructuring and reorganization to move talent to the emerging markets to ensure key players and supporting teams are deployed in the most active markets (ie east of Cairo). Looking forward to the next five to 10 years, many predict construction will change significantly. This will involve moving from predominately in-situ build to off-site, precast production with assembly on site. This will demand new thinking and new skills with less labour on site to pour concrete but more skilled technicians to complete the build.

FIGURE 5.1 Infrastructure growth by region

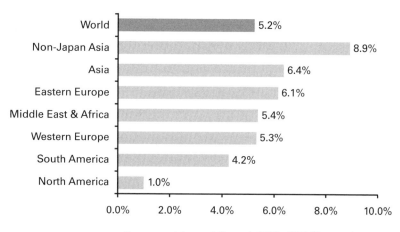

Compound Annual Growth 2008–2013 (Percent)

SOURCE: Global Construction Outlook (IHS Global Insight)

TABLE 5.2 Construction spending by region

	Total Construction Spending 2005 US$ Billions	Total Real Construction Spending Growth 2005 US$		
	2009	Growth % 2008–2009	Growth % 2009–2010	Growth, CAGR % 2008–2013
China	701.6	+9.9%	+9.8%	+9.5%
Australia	135.6	+4.8%	+4.9%	+5.1%
Indonesia	82.0	+4.7%	+6.7%	+5.5%
India	214.8	+4.4%	+7.0%	+7.2%
Bangladesh	14.9	+4.0%	+5.3%	+5.8%
Qatar	5.5	+3.8%	+0.2%	+3.4%
South Africa	32.1	+3.4%	+5.9%	+5.6%
Parama	2.9	+3.0%	+6.6%	+7.1%
Vietnam	7.6	+3.0%	+3.6%	+4.5%
Thailand	21.8	+2.6%	+4.4%	+4.5%
Saudi Arabia	58.6	+2.4%	+5.2%	+5.3%
Kenya	2.4	+1.7%	+4.7%	+5.2%
South Korea	157.4	+1.4%	+4.3%	+2.3%
Poland	66.8	+1.3%	+2.2%	+3.4%
Sweden	37.5	+1.0%	+2.4%	+3.4%
69 Country Total	5,565.0	(−3.7%)	+0.7%	+2.3%

SOURCE: *Global Construction Insight*[4]

From a workforce viewpoint, the redeployment of very senior staff to the new markets reflects a need to position very experienced (sector- and project-specific staff) as leaders of any bid team (Baby Boomers become born-again nomads!) plus clear ability to deploy a fully experienced team able to start on time and follow through on the work. Hence there is a greater emphasis on ensuring organizations have the right people in place to deliver projects. This is also critical from a risk-reduction perspective.

Whilst there are more people in the marketplace, the reality is that all main firms have approached this recession in a different light: rather than make across-the-board reductions, they have been very selective in identifying who are critical talents that the firm needs to keep; there has been a deliberate move to keep the best talent. This means that whilst there may be quantity on the market, the skill and competency levels are lower.

Going after the new talent also poses some challenges. In the past, the industry held on to talent through its generous final salary pension plans. Most companies have abandoned these for new joiners and Generations X and Y are not interested anyway. Senior staff say there is a noticeable shift in attitude of the new workforce, to whom companies will need to offer a different proposition.

The implication is clear, China, India, Brazil and Mexico will be the growth markets in the next five to 10 years – but at least two of the major economic commentators have admitted they have not really looked at Central and Latin America yet and they see Eastern Europe and India as 'problematic'.

The lack of local expertise in specialist skills, business acumen and leadership also means the nomads are likely to have much greater delegation of authority and resulting accountability much earlier in their careers. As a result, younger professionals can progress rapidly within existing organizations or use this success to leverage their employability to other firms. This has two consequences: first, organizations come under significant pressure to promote professionals in emerging markets faster than elsewhere, creating perceived inconsistencies in grading; and second, the nomads tend to have unrealistic expectations of their value and career prospects in situ. All of which fuels the higher attrition and mobility of the nomadic professional.

For the Generation Y nomad, this is simply water off a duck's back; with a shrug of the shoulders they will be off to pastures new and another adventure. They are quite comfortable with change; they are highly adaptable and can deal with ambiguity or paradox since they are confident self-starters. A 'correction' or adjustment in their work career just means that they need to reach out to their widening digital network.

Workplace attitude, norms and business reality

Unlike previous generations, this is not a group who are concerned with how long a task takes or how many activities are documented on their job description.

> I like that it is project based and the people that I work with. The office has a lot of well-educated and experienced colleagues that I feel I can learn from.

> The variation of people I interact with (internally and externally), being involved with research and development, using what I learn and having the sense that there are tangible results and input is having an impact.

> I like that I get more freedom here and I'm given independence to do things my way.

> I like the fact that we are rotating through the different business offerings – I like being exposed to all these different lines. I also like working with lots of different people and leaders from lots of different backgrounds who give different perspectives and ideas.

> The diversity of work – this is always the most important factor for me. Working with such a range of nationalities and working in a market that is less mature, it always provides people of my age group more opportunities: more senior roles, higher exposure and greater opportunities. I also like the travel element of it.

> The job is geographically diverse, it is intellectually challenging – the clients we advise have not got clear grasps so we are able to invent and innovate new ideas. We are creating good new intellectual capital. There is also the diversity of the people that you deal with – lots of different nationalities with locals and expats together.

> I get lots of opportunities here to work with clients and get hands-on experience. I like the make-up of the office – the office is young but with some older guys who are always happy to help and help you develop your career. I like the responsibility that I'm given.

And unlike Generation X, they are not so ambitious that they want to impress their boss by being the first into work and last out of the door. They do not expect to clock in or record their time. They will plan and organize their day to the task in hand. If that means staying until midnight to complete the task, that's fine provided it's recognized and it's occasional. The balance between life and work is more fluid. This is a change from the Traditionalists, Baby Boomers and some Generation X managers who want highly structured, controlled workdays where internal meetings are booked, everyone is on time, ready and prepared, agendas are followed, actions agreed and an internal report is produced stating the meeting has been completed and everything is in hand. Generation Y see this as simply bosses covering their backsides.

Their more relaxed working pattern in part mirrors the commercial world of the emerging markets where customer and client meetings are less predictable. Appointments are made but invariably subject to delay as previous appointments overrun; attendees are not guaranteed to be there (last-minute apologies); agendas are fluid and conversations will drift into major cul-de-sacs; and presentations are often more about information sharing than decision points.

This creates a tension and degree of stress for the new nomad. Western multinationals are still trying to operate a business model driven on focused, systematic outcomes whilst the reality of business in the emerging markets is more ambiguous, where customers and clients deliberately leave terms or conversations loose, open for debate and further negotiation.

For the new nomad, a key skill is the ability to handle these difficult conversations and conflicting goals whilst remaining at ease to work within broad frameworks, authority matrices and potentially to work outside the strict rules. This gives the new nomad a need for risk and 'edginess' that push the boundaries without drawing too much corporate attention. In most cases the major corporates recognize this reality and are prepared to relax some of the rules provided codes of business propriety are not conflicted. For some functions, now strengthened by the retrenchment, this is difficult and leads to further demands for internal monitoring and reporting.

There will continue to be cases where these commercial tensions are pushed to the limit. The Leeson affair epitomized the worst abuse. Nick Leeson was the chief trader in Asia for Baring Brothers, the UK investment bank operating out of Singapore. His daredevil deals were spectacular, creating phenomenal revenues. However, the corporate governance above Leeson was flawed, so that the financial rewards (ie short-term bonuses) that he 'earned' where mirrored in payments to his superiors. The ultimate crash brought the house down.[5] The recent financial scandal at Société Générale involving trader Jerome Kerviel exposed similar issues in an alleged US$ 7.1 billion fraud.[6]

The difference, for the future, is that the very nature of work has changed. It will be more collaborative, hopefully with more transparency and a higher level of trust. Whilst the mature countries have implemented increased regulation and monitoring of financial systems, the real change will come in a new mindset for employers and employees. Generation Y and the nomads can provide this impetus. They carry a greater sense of optimism for a globally engaged group with wider, communal goals rather than pure monetary gain. The multinationals will need to overhaul their recognition and reward systems to match this enthusiasm with a new workplace proposition.

Where next – which location?

The vast majority of those interviewed in Dubai were clear that they would be moving on partly for career and more to live in another city of the world. Only those with extended families living in Dubai and with young children were going to stay and even then for four to five years when secondary education would kick in.

> Not in Dubai, probably in an English-speaking country such as the US or Australia – depends on what opportunities arise but will try to take proactive actions to move to preferred destinations.
>
> Hungarian Generation Y

> I certainly don't think I'll be in Dubai, I'm open to exploring other locations, I see myself living in another part of the world. I would say that it is more about the experience than career progression, but it I'd like to learn about other business markets and get business acumen.
>
> Lebanese Generation X

> In thee years I would like to do something similar in Brazil or elsewhere in Latin America.
>
> British Baby Boomer

> Still overseas, Singapore and Hong Kong are top of our list. We will still be working and pursuing careers. The main criterion is that the jobs must be interesting and challenging roles to develop and fulfil us. It must also work for the children, so provision of good-quality education would be a must. Eventually we shall go back to the UK but I am quite worried about how easy it might be – I have seen other expats struggle to return. It may be more difficult to make new friends, especially with people who cannot relate to our experiences.
>
> British Generation X

> I am debating this in my mind – not Dubai, that's guaranteed. If I could choose, it would be New York.
>
> Portuguese Generation Y / Generation X

> My next step will feed into my career path – a higher role. I am happy to be loyal so long as they have something to offer in exchange and interest in me is taken – don't want to be loyal for nothing.
>
> Iraqi Generation Y

Having experienced the transient nature of Dubai, most have their sights on more established cities – Hong Kong, Singapore, Sydney, New York or London. All of these are still expat centres and very cosmopolitan, international and multicultural.

I think nomads gravitate towards other nomads – networks of nomads exist. It is their behaviours, pursuits, level of challenge and friendships that define nomads from others. Nomads exist in hundreds of cities in the world in many different services.

Australian Baby Boomer

I wonder whether I will be tired of this kind of lifestyle and travelling in the future, but currently I am not. I could see myself possibly living in Hong Kong.

Polish Generation X

I want to visit as many new places as I can and will retire somewhere in South-east Asia with an aim to be part-time teaching at a university.

Venezuelan Baby Boomer

I want to do lots of Asian travel first; more time in Australia and build a holiday house in Sri Lanka with Provence, France as an occasional base.

English Baby Boomer

I see myself in Australia or somewhere else in Asia where I can live comfortably but have the opportunity to work throughout Asia.

Bangladeshi Generation Y

What is missing, of course, are all the other major cities of the world like Paris, Berlin, Rome, Madrid, Los Angeles, Moscow or Delhi. For this group these are holiday destinations for sightseeing and culture but lack the draw of internationalism.

Living offshore had given us a real insight into how we wanted to live our lives. We found safety, stability and security in Australia but not challenge. We found predictability – and often what makes life interesting is unpredictability. This level of unpredictability is really exciting for us. I am encouraged by my wife, not held back – there's an important message about support mechanisms.

Australian Generation X

I'd like to try North America, otherwise perhaps somewhere else in Europe or Hong Kong. I'd like to live and work in a big international city.

Italian Generation X

Not surprisingly, most have a wish for family at some point. Those with children already are most concerned as to their future. Part of the attraction of Dubai and Singapore seems to be the degree of safety these states can offer given crime rates are virtually non-existent. London and New York fall down in this respect yet remain attractive to the single or non-kid nomads.

For many, as we have seen, their childhood was spent moving from one location to another because of their father's job. And whilst some women say they are prepared to go where their husband goes, a rising number are more interested in where they want to bring up their current or future children.

> The children of nomads hang out together – have similar experiences, eg kids will happily travel on a plane for six hours – at seven my daughter wants to live in New York, I didn't even know where New York was when I was that age; my five-year-old can speak two languages fluently and goes to school with kids that speak four languages. European kids also usually speak three languages. We are driven by where we want our kids to grow up and give them stability when they are teenagers – have seen families go off the rails because they were forced to move where their dad wanted.

It also raises an interesting question as to the next generation to appear – Generation Z or whatever. The conclusion from the insights above is that most of the nomads were already nomadic at a very young age, either following their parents around due to work or their parents' love of travelling for both culture or exotic holidays. Generation Z children will be even more global minded, adventurous and naturally skilled in language and social skills.

A quarter of these New nomads want to set up their own business – many in retail or a restaurant.

> Ten years is a long time from now. I do hope that I am healthy enough and have the means to continue to travel and visit new countries; it is something that I am passionate about. If I do have my own family, I'd want to make sure that they are exposed to the world in the same way that I was, growing up. There is only so much you can learn from a textbook, you have to actually get out there and experience life to learn anything.

> We shall probably go back to the US so our children can be closer to their grandparents. I would like to start up my own business but most of all I will want to live abroad so my children can have the experience of learning another language proficiently during their teens. We will probably take them on a great road trip from cape to cape in Africa or across the US. I think we shall retire to Buenos Aires.

> Ella knows she was born in China – and she has a Chinese name – the characters are a particularly clever usage by friends of ours, and it basically means 'Dad's little heart' – and she thinks it's really cool. When we ate Chinese noodles in a little backstreet noodle shop when we moved back to Sydney, Ella was the hit of the restaurant's Chinese owners because she was a Beijing baby. Because Katarina was born in Australia she wants to learn how to surf. Ella feels more German as she is much more like Kirsten – that's it. The others are too young. We are very keen to show them cultures, countries and languages so they know where they

come from – sort of. The thing about Dubai is that *all* their friends are like they are. Multiple languages, multiple cities/homes, and parents from different nationalities – 12 nationalities in Ella's class; 14 in Katarina's. And so this is normal to them. We take them to Germany and to Australia and they love it because of their cousins and families, etc, but they want to get back to their friends. Home is where Mum and Dad are, I suppose. They have cousins in Hamburg, Atlanta and Brisbane. They know all three cities. Their grandparents live in Hamburg and Launceston and they speak in the appropriate languages to all of them each weekend. Katarina says 'grass' like a South African would because one of her friends comes from there; they sang 'Happy Birthday' in Arabic to my 81-year-old mother this year and it had her in tears. Another friend is Scottish – so she dances highland dancing in a group of seven-year-olds where there's a girl called Fatima! Gotta love that. All of them have dual citizenship. Ella's passport is issued in London, Katarina's in Sydney, mine in Beijing, Kirsten's German passport is from Melbourne, Tommy's from London and Paul is getting his next week in Dubai.

An Emirati viewpoint

Dubai remains unique as the first modern city to be built to attract the professional nomad. Along with Abu Dhabi, its federal neighbour and rising competitor city, both are part of the seven Emirates which formed the Arab state in 1970. The United Arab Emirates is a success story in a region of upheaval, conflict and tribal tension.

There are some 850,000 Emiratis in a resident population of over 6 million; hence 85 per cent of those living in Dubai are expats from all corners of the world – most from well-established cities.[7] Dubai with its goal of technology modernity has transformed a desert port into a towering city of steel and glass.

The Emiratis are desperately seeking their identity, wanting to preserve their language, religion and culture. But like modern organizations the country is struggling with the pace of change whilst living with four generations. It has gone from Bedouin to modernity but unlike its Saudi neighbour has committed itself to a philosophy of 'making business work'. The pace of development has prevented detailed debate. The population is growing fast – 60 per cent are aged under 25; in fact, 10 per cent are aged under 15.[8] This again is not unusual in emerging markets.[9] There is a huge issue brewing in respect of the younger generation who have been exposed to travel, the internet, international brands, communication and fashion. The government, a benign autocracy, is controlling power through regulation.

Arabic culture is not only fascinating but runs very deep in society. Arabian Gulf names, for example, are complicated constructs, DNAs of history, and include the following: a family name (*Kunya*) which usually reflects the birthplace, profession, descendents or tribe (*Qabela*) of the great-grandfathers or ancestors. The tribe in some cases is not mentioned in the written or spoken name but would be stated on the passport under the *Qabela* category. Some have a second name; son of X (*Ibn X*) that is needed for identifying the father of the person. This is due to the habit of renaming children after their grandparents where some names are repeated many times in a family and could lead to having cousins carrying the exact same names. A first name (*Ism*) – which reflects a meaning or historical links, and may be prefaced by either *Sayyed* (descendant of the Prophet) or *Sheik* (royal ruling or significant family). Luckily these names are usually shortened to three names. A generic example would be Amer Hameed Al Mansoori, also nicknamed Abu Ahmad Al Mansoori (father of Ahmad Al Mansoori). This fellow's full name is Amer Ibn Hameed Ibn Mohammed Al Mansoori. In this name Amer is the *Ism* (first name). *Ibn* Hameed means son of Hameed; therefore, Hameed is the father and Mohammed is the grandfather, and Al Mansoori is the tribe or *Qabela*, which is the last name in this example. Hence my short nickname would be Abu Miles Matthewman! All names have a meaning, often preceded by Abdul (meaning 'worshipper or servant of God') plus one of 99 adjectives describing the Prophet Mohammed such as Abdul Rahman ('worshipper of the Merciful One').

The Arabic language has 28 letters with no *p*, *v*, *ga* or *ch* sounds. Classical Arabic is written and very formal and therefore spoken Arabic has many dialects and differs by country, although Egyptian and Syrian are good reference points, as these two dialects are easy to understand due to being the most prominent dialects on television in the Middle East.

There are strong etiquettes in respect of dress, greetings, coffee ceremony, seating arrangements and the importance of the right hand (I was immediately identified as a leftie!). All of which is crucial cultural information for nomads wanting to do business in this key region – and, more importantly, an indication of the detail multinationals need to make as core within diversity and multicultural training, not just for their global nomads but also for those interfacing with them at head office.

A prominent Emirati illustrated this wonderfully with the concept of '*In Sha Allah*'. This literally means 'God willing' and is used extensively in conversation since Arabs cannot predict the future as this is only in God's will. Second, as a faith that finds it very difficult to say no, '*In Sha Allah*' becomes a convenient way of saying 'yes', 'maybe' or 'no' – depending on the inflexion. Thus a Western executive can easily be frustrated in asking a local Emirati 'to prepare a report on my desk by 9 am' with the response of '*In Sha Allah*'. Demanding that God should not be part of the discussion is not acceptable as Islam sets the context for all daily life, at home or at work. This is where Western firms must do more to educate senior and middle managers in the way of doing business as trade moves east of Cairo.

But like the city, Emirati life is transient. The modernity is feeding generational change. A city half-filled in terms of apartment and office occupancy will need to attract a new generation of business to survive. In the world of recovery where the bubble of real estate, high-income tourism and financial risk has been blown apart, the city will have to seek out more innovation, new entrepreneurs and a new vibrancy.

The balance between inputs and outputs is very different in the Emirates. The focus is all around development needs with unlimited access to education, driving progress and ability to change.

Yet, unlike other emerging markets of India, China or Brazil, there is no mass workforce to manufacture consumer goods; there is no semi-skilled technical workforce to fashion machine tools; instead there is an educated professional group destined to manage others but without the work ethic, given the benign entitlement culture of the Emirati state.

Like their nomadic population, the Emiratis have realized that it is difficult to build friendships and that relationships are transitory. But unlike their visitors, many have retreated to their own, unwilling to invest the time, trying to preserve and keep alive their heritage.

Whilst the power of Islam will remain a powerful force throughout the wider community, the extended family and daily life sets the context of business life. The state is struggling to keep pace with the demands of Generations X and Y. It is likely their next generation will also become nomadic and will seek alternative experiences with international firms.

Perspectives from other cities

There are, of course, many cities of the world that have attracted professional nomads over the years and remain destination centres for the new-generation workforce. London, New York, Hong Kong, Shanghai, Singapore, Sydney, Hyderabad and Mumbai are all competing for this new talent. But each has a particular draw.

London

The UK, and London in particular, is a top choice for graduate and post-graduate education and a second job move for young professionals. Its main draw is clearly the English language, which allows many young from former English colonies – New Zealand, Australia, America, Hong Kong – a common base in which to be understood. It also provides a richness of history and culture throughout the ages from Roman to medieval to Victorian and modern times. More recently Generation X and Generation Y offspring of the ever-expanding European Union have benefited from early introduction to English as a second language, plus the expansion of free movement and freedom of labour. From the 1960s to the 'Cool Britannia' of the 1990s, the liberalization of the press plus the lively pop and nightlife scene have acted as a magnate for changing fashions in the arts. This has added colour and vibrancy to the city. London remains a city where travellers can find any type of restaurant, bar or music taste.

London is a truly global city on a par with New York; it's 'Fundon', a city full of entertainment, thriving nightlife and something for everyone.

American Generation X

London has easy access to sport with a landscape of bars that are always changing.

Generation Y banker

The sheer number of choices is what makes London unique. It didn't matter if I was in the mood for Chinese, Italian, Indian or Lebanese food, I could always find a wide variety of fantastic restaurants in every price range.

Canadian Generation X

London is cosmopolitan, has great entertainment and a good job market with easy access to other major cities in Europe. It is so expensive to go back home and with friends scattered throughout Brazil, it is easier for my parents and friends to come to England; more fun too!

Brazilian Generation X

London is an amazing city where you can find everything in terms of things to do, things to buy, things to see and people to meet. The cultural offer is fantastic and it is the best restaurant city in the world.

Swedish Generation X

London is very metropolitan; it is a talent magnet for financial services. There are things to do 24/7. It's multicultural, which I love. It's close to other places – you can fly anywhere in Europe relatively fast and cheaply.

Swedish Generation X / Generation Y

As children we would often stop over in London. It was a city I had grown to love and I knew that someday I would like to live there. I was hesitant about moving away from friends. London to me was a cultural melting pot, a place where I could hear 10 different languages as I walked down a street. I love the diversity. Oddly, it made me feel at home.

Pakistani Generation Y

Britain has not only encouraged trading across many parts of the world but also in recent years has operated an open, tolerant policy to immigrants and refugees, allowing a free-flowing mix of race, religion and customs.

It's a city without borders, full of variety on a scale with which few others can compare.

Heathrow and its sister airports, the Channel Tunnel and sheer proximity to Europe also mean that London is a convenient hub to discover the breadth of Europe; again aided by the advent of cheap air, coach and train travel.

But unlike Singapore and Dubai, the city has a safety problem for many. Its freedoms have allowed militant groups to use its international focus to mount protest movements and violent campaigns across a wide range of agendas. The continual influx of tourists (it is estimated that 27 million visit London each year), provide organized crime gangs the cover to operate in drugs, prostitution, pornography, money laundering and counterfeit goods, which in turn can create local crime issues that hit the international press – for example, the torture and murder of two French students for their credit cards and computers. But for some global nomads, notably from the Muslim world, London can be too threatening. Ironically, for Brazilians coming from Rio and São Paulo, London is seen as a safe city where there is less likelihood of being mugged in the evenings!

Second, the sheer concentration of people and a lack of open spaces, the high cost of living and lack of high-quality schooling mean there is a group of the new nomads who will continue to opt out of London as a choice of pre-college schooling for their children. For these couples, the international schools of the emerging markets can offer a distinct advantage – their offspring will discover the cosmopolitan cities of London and elsewhere in later life. In the meantime, the UK capital and the great cities of Europe are places to visit for sightseeing and short-break holidays.

London is also very cliquey. Because it is so large, many nomads in London will gravitate to their own – the New Zealanders go to 'The Church' in Euston; the Australians head for Walkabout, the Greeks for Fitzroy Square; and the Brazilians for the tapas bars of Charing Cross.

But London's biggest downside is its cost of living – in 2008 it was estimated to be the most expensive city in the world, although this has now dropped.

> It has very high costs of living and appalling housing standards. It is always congested and you have to book in advance. The infrastructure is a hassle – public transport is unreliable; roads are poor quality and there is generally bad customer service for UK consumer companies (banks, phone companies, travel agencies, etc).

> On the negative side, it's very stressful, dirty, and the people are rather unhealthy – lots of drinking and pub culture with not much exercise and unhealthy food. It is very expensive.

> London has a steep learning curve when it comes to familiarizing yourself – for example, knowing where to live and how much to pay for rent, and learning the language – I didn't realize how different British English is from American.

London has now slipped down to 21st, with Oslo, Zurich, Copenhagen, Geneva and Tokyo occupying the top five positions. However, this also meant for certain professions the salaries were the highest in the world and can be used to leverage promotions or future careers.

Hong Kong

The city remains a favoured destination for many expats and new nomads. Since the handover from Britain to China it has changed but not as much as some had feared. Many corporate headquarters are still based there – the exodus to Taiwan and other places has not happened and, in fact, Hong Kong has become an Asian regional hub as the door to China in addition to its own business centre. Hence, arguably, it has grown in importance.

It is a magnet for nomads in the financial services, manufacturing and consumer goods markets, although with its access to the New Territories of China nearly every industry sector is represented. Hence, Hong Kong attracts a mix of professions plus government and business administration and, of course, these skills are highly portable.

Its stock market remains strong and attractive to 'red chairs' – ie local firms looking to raise funds for expansion – and more recently to others for alternative listings to London or New York. It offers high rates of pay and low taxation. Unlike its competitors, Hong Kong boasts many corporate headquarters and so its expat population has been more stable with a tendency to stay. But there is now a growing trend of Hong Kong being used to 'blood' the new nomads before a posting to Shanghai.

For most, Hong Kong offers a fabulous mix – matching weather, waterfront and beaches, with exotic culture plus vibrant nightlife. It is cosmopolitan, has a laissez-faire buzz and strong English language roots, and is a sophisticated city with strong traditions of trading with Britain and the West, which makes it an easy place in which to do business. Its business folk also have the reputation of cutting a deal quickly and moving on, unlike some other locations. In this respect it remains easier than Taiwan or Soeul, even down to a high proportion of taxi drivers understanding English. Its transport infrastructure is first class and cheap (unlike London and Singapore).

The standard of living is very good, with many traditional expats enjoying lifestyles beyond those in their native home country – notably packages including club membership, domestic help, private health plans and private education. Unlike some other nomadic cities, the education system is well established, so families are comfortable to consider both primary and secondary education within Hong Kong as it can cater to UK, US, Swiss, French and German standards.

What is different is that most foreign school leavers (and upwardly mobile local Chinese) seek out universities in the UK, Australia and the United States and then return for their first serious job. The job market, relatively cheap standard of living and accessibility make it attractive. It is also considered a safe city.

Unlike Dubai, its expat population is well settled with a mix between short-term transferees and long-standing corporate professionals working in the corporate HQs. More are likely to say they are French, English or German and whilst there are 'national zones', a high number will still say Hong Kong is 'home'.

There is still a tendency for new nomads and expats to seek out their own kin, partly because they remain the minority in a Chinese city. Indeed, there are well-established social clubs such as the Bangkok Club, the St Andrew's Society, Landmark, Aberdeen Boat Club, Aviation Club (pilots, of course), Clearwater Bay Golf Club and East India Club, but in the main there is a high degree of integration within the expat and nomad communities because of 'club culture'. Given the Asian emphasis on seniority, some of these reflect both social and business hierarchies.

In the past, corporates typically offered salary and housing allowances with the express terms of rental (thereby keeping next move options open). These positions have now changed with many organizations giving a housing allowance but not specifying how it is used. This has meant more established expats using these allowances to subsidize buying accommodation and, hence, a commitment to the city.

Singapore

The city state of Singapore has recently been voted as offering the best quality of life.[10] This is largely because most of its construction is now complete and yet it has managed to preserve significant greenery and amenities. It is renowned for its cleanliness, lack of crime and demand for ultra-efficiency. As one nomad said, 'It's Asia with plumbing.'

> Singapore is well organized and well managed. Currently I am living a hassle-free life. After 10 years of work in four separate countries, I think I am quite nomadic.

> Singapore is a great international city; it is Asia-lite, so you have the benefits of working in Asia but it's clean, safe and efficient and great for families. It is amazing for travel as you can be in so many cool countries in less than three hours, especially with the competition of budget airlines – there are lots of inexpensive flights to every destination.

Whilst the weather and waterfront are good (a feature of all the nomadic cities), it can be very humid.

> It has terrible drivers and taxis whose English or map orientation is poor. The malls are always crowded – I prefer to shop elsewhere.

> Singapore is perfect – I am closer to my home (India); it has the same climate but far less corruption and a good political system – my parents have come to live near me.

Singapore is an easy, clean, safe regional centre. Has great food, good shopping but I miss sports. The censorship and control of the press make the city too square and boring – a pity.

Singapore is a place where expats will either be bored in three months or will stay for ever – it is not that exciting; there is a lack of sporting facilities. There is censorship and the whole way of life centres around eating, shopping and the cinema.

I am fitter than ever before – I eat more fish than meat. Shopping is easy and there are loads of bars but I miss the fun and sense of community – there is no real ' craic' here. The time difference with other locations is a real hassle.

Singapore has become a business hub, replacing Hong Kong with more multinational companies setting up regional offices here. It is a place to be but it is a bit monotonous and boring. I guess the country is too small. So most of the time I look to visiting the neighbouring countries to explore their natural resources.

The city provides a mix of nationalities on neutral ground; variety of Asian cuisines and is free of 'big city' constraints, for example, lack of home space, difficulty in parking, decent offices and a hassle-free airport.

For those slightly older nomads, especially in the technology, oil industry, financial services and, more recently, generic pharmaceuticals industries, Singapore offers tax-free income for five years, international schooling, an easy lifestyle with great access to other exotic places. Those with families they can invest in their future and for those nomads who are either single or a couple it provides a step change for three years before moving on to the next destination. The main issue is that the economy is very volatile, so when times are good life is buoyant but as soon as there is a dip, foreign manual labour and expats are let go very quickly.

Hyderabad and Mumbai

These thriving Indian cities have become major hubs linking international travel to regional cities of the Asian subcontinent as well as becoming the booming high-tech, cyber-city and financial centres.

Yet neither is a major expat city or centre for global nomads. This is because India has adopted restrictive visa regulations. As a result, in Mumbai there is only a small expat community of British, Dutch and French, which, combined with the monsoon and high humidity, makes the city less attractive for both the nomad and importantly any partner.

To survive, the nomad needs to come to terms with the monsoon weather, the state of the roads – and they must love cricket.

But younger, more adventurous nomads are exploring cities like Mumbai and look forward to living and working there to get the experience of working in a thriving financial hub and a developing country. Whilst they come to terms with the infrastructure, pollution and crowds, the fast-paced life of the city and especially the exciting night life hold them to the place for a few years till they are ready to settle and have a family.

Hyderabad as a city has attracted the older, more settled nomad who is looking for a better quality of life. The biggest sector that has looked for nomads in this city is the IT and technology sector. Global expats who have shifted to Hyderabad have appreciated the quiet pace of life, the cleanliness and the relative greenery compared with Mumbai. However, Hyderabad is still not a truly international city and some of the related amenities and sense of community may be missing for such people to think of it as a longer-term destination.

Usage of expats and nomads differs markedly between industries. The manufacturing and technology-led industries have used expats sparingly, mainly for operational leadership and knowledge transfer of critical processes; and most notably for start-up operations. There is a strong appreciation of and respect for legal professionals and the civil service. Indian managers are highly capable, hence there is less need for expats than in China or Korea.

In the main, Indian industry tends to feel that market leadership requires sufficient understanding of the uniqueness of the local market. But there are a few exceptions, notably airline pilots and top-class chefs. Otherwise the hot skills tend to be centred around particular technologies or industry-specific processes.

India, of course, offers huge opportunities and remains a great place to do business but as the recovery takes hold so the labour market is becoming more mobile (internally and externally). India remains one of the largest exporters of talent across the world.

Shanghai

Shanghai would be considered a fairly young city of 150 years compared with many around the world and in China especially. It grew out of the international treaties and concessions following the Opium Wars in 1856. In the 1920s and 1930s it became known as 'the Paris of the East'. Consequently it has a strong climate of commerce matched with a spirit of entrepreneurialism. Like Hong Kong, its inhabitants and companies have been keen to cut a deal quickly. However, it has also shown itself to be politically astute, with many of China's modern leaders coming from the city.

It has benefited from modern planning. In 2010 the city will host the World Expo with an estimated half million visitors each day. Whilst it is heavily polluted, the authorities will be able to cope.

The city has a strong mix of Taiwanese, Japanese, German, British and French expat communities, along with 'ABCs' (American-born Chinese).

From 2002 to 2004 there was a huge shift in focus. The influx of businesses expected from Hong Kong did not happen. Instead the vacuum was picked up by Korean firms hungry for talent. To match the demand from the USA and UK, there has been a rising demand for expat managers and specialists. These older, more experienced nomads (screened out by the visa process) allowed local firms to step up to provide added-value products and services, enabling significant penetration into the US market.

An interesting evolution post-global crisis (and now the Dubai situation) is that given China's strong performance during this down cycle, local companies are looking to evolve their operational model with more of a focus on North Asia. Some Eastern companies in Japan and Korea have made their major acquisitions and overseas operations in Europe and North America due to the advanced nature of business there. But now there is an accelerated shift and refocus on China.

What is happening now is that the visa process is again being used to screen for specific skills and rather than employ expats on costly international assignments, firms (Western multinationals and local) are looking to localize contracts.

Tokyo

The city of Tokyo symbolizes Japan's incredible consumer economy. It remains a magnet for nomads given its extraordinary opportunities and corresponding attitude of 'can do'. It has a significant stock market and as such attracts expats specializing in major deals, corporate financiers, lawyers, consultants and financial services, along with IT wizards.

Whilst the city pulsates with millions of commuters every day and the constant flow of bodies on trains, metros, buses and cars into offices and shops at any time of the day, it remains easy to escape into the countryside, to the beauty and spas of Kyoto or Sapporo. Life for an expat is very expensive but Tokyo can conjure any lifestyle theme to match anything elsewhere in the world.

Bangkok

This city acts as a regional outpost and transport hub to the wider Thai peninsula plus the added advantage of good relationships with China and the Japanese. The country's workforce is energetic and has a good level of education with high numeracy and English literacy. It is an easy place for manufacturing but lacks depth in the tertiary industries of professional services.

The city is congested and there is a nervousness about the political instability. However, this is not an impediment to doing business. Expats just need to stay clear. The people are always smiling but they are dangerous to cross or upset; they do not like losing, so win–win negotiations are critical. Nomads must also show respect to the monks and the royal family.

The benefits are that there is wonderful culture, great food and an affordable, good level of housing.

> For the expats, community life is very comfortable – the nomads fall into the group aged late 20s or 30s who are seeking out the Thai experience whilst there is another group aged late 50s to 70s who have had broken marriages and found a new life with a Thai partner and have accepted the full family and community obligations that are expected.

Sydney

Sydney is a favoured, next-stop destination for many of the younger nomads. The city is not only a magnet for international travellers but also internally within Australia. It is picturesque, with the ferry carrying commuters to and fro across the harbour, and it boasts a strong outdoor lifestyle centred around beaches and parks.

It is the country's financial capital and has many major corporates based in the centre. The Australian dollar is one of the top five or six most traded currencies. The city attracts IT, technology and transport professionals.

For the transient nomad, the buzz and multicultural colour of the city is very attractive but for longer stayers the capital is seen as a little superficial with only narrow belts offering the dream (harbour land and the Northern Line). Elsewhere the level of pollution is high and congestion is proving a nightmare for traffic.

References

1 100 global nomads interviewed by Jim and Miles Matthewman, August–December 2009
2 'A new world order – how the G8 became the G20', www.theroot.com/new-world-order, 24 September 2009
3 Mohammed El-Erian, 'The new normal', www.pimco.com/SecularOutlook, May 2009
4 'Global construction outlook', IHS Global Insight
5 Nick Leeson (1997) Rogue Trader, Warner, London
6 'Fraud costs French bank $7.1 billion', New York Times, 25 January 2008
7 globalisation.inquirer.net/news/breakingnews/view/20080224-120926/Influx-of-expats-boosts-UAE-population-report
8 Ibid
9 Emerging markets population figure
10 Mercer Quality of Life Index, 2009

PART THREE
The challenge for multinationals

Introduction

The multinational giants have a problem. As the evidence in Part One shows, the bet is on in respect of the emerging markets for the source of economic recovery and growth. The mature domestic markets will struggle to recover to stimulate home demand and are likely to require substantial restructuring. This will take between five and 10 years to embed.

Part Three looks at why doing business is different in the developing and emerging markets and the implications for the mobile and local workforces from a multinational corporate point of view.

Some commentators are already predicting and seeing the early signs of a talent flight. But the issues run much deeper. The impact of the switch in focus to the emerging markets will demand organizational redesign, workforce reconstruction (ie more than restructuring), fundamental leadership change both in constitution and mindset and, more importantly, the assumptions embodied in career plans and reward.

How global are the major firms?

06

Henry Kissinger once said: 'The problem with globalization is that not everyone wants to be an American.'

For the past 10 years, we have been bombarded by the predominant American philosophy that in a growth economy, globalization is the key goal. But what exactly do we understand by the term 'globalization'? In simple terms it is the widening, deepening and pace of global connections.

But for most the term is seen as economic integration characterized by Western capitalism, free trade principles with minimal national interference, epitomized by the 2010 stand-off between Google and the Chinese government. The image is one of organizations operating independently of national boundaries. It is also portrayed as a 'good thing' and almost inevitable. But as the World Bank stated in 2000:

> Tremendous advances have been made by large segments of the world population in this age of globalization. Yet there is a fear that globalization is exacerbating inequality, and perhaps even worsening the lot of the poor by eroding their incomes, increasing their vulnerability, and adding to their disempowerment.[1]

Likewise, Greenpeace in 1999 defined globalization as 'a global framework of law, policy and institutions that will create a more balanced global economy with sustainable impacts on the environment and natural resources, and that will benefit all people in a fairer, more equitable way'.[2]

But globalization is not new – there have always been international flows of trade. What is different is that whilst the pace and amount of trade being undertaken have multiplied, paradoxically many multinational firms tend to reflect their home countries.

Very few firms are truly global – a handful of organizations can claim this title: Coca-Cola, Doosan (the Korean conglomerate), PricewaterhouseCoopers (although this is more like a federation of firms under a marketing banner), Volkswagen; McDonald's though it's franchising brand. They may operate in three or four continents but many ignore Africa or Latin America. What is new is that national economies have to work as a unit at the world level in real time. This gives a tremendous advantage to multinational firms, since they already have the knowledge required to produce and market goods and services internationally. If only they maximized the knowledge from a global, multicultural mindset!

As Figure 6.1 shows, there is still a huge Western bias in the distribution of Western multinationals – 56 per cent according to Forbes (which strongly accords with the FTSE 500 global firms) but the message is clear: there has been a huge switch to the Pacific Rim in the last five years, accelerating in the last two.

Some major global brands have failed to conquer all major markets (for example in Saudi Arabia, Coca-Cola is not recognized but Pepsi is) – they basically define the world in their own terms. I remember consulting to a major pharmaceutical firm whose corporate mission was to be number one in the world but when challenged, given they only had 40 per cent market share, answered that the world was defined as everywhere except China (which had over 50 per cent of their particular market). Likewise, Vodafone's ambitions do not quite match their aspirational global status as analysts claim that they have failed to conquer the US market, although their joint venture with Verizon has proved highly profitable.

In reality, I find most major multinational firms are actually *international*. They typically operate in three or four continents, perhaps in 40 or so countries, but are very focused on their key markets. Some openly admit to being focused on specific English-speaking markets, high-growth markets or low-risk markets. Few actively target countries to develop new markets for long-term development or to alleviate poverty or create social change even though these are the stated goals or principles of politicians, some corporates and Generation Y.

So whilst the term globalization is primarily used to describe economic trade, internationalism is more often a descriptor of politics, social and cultural trends. Perhaps we need to define this language in the 'new normal' world. Indeed, the United Nations has said:

> At the global level, there is a need to question the current governance structures, ie the United Nations agencies, the Bretton Woods institutions (the World Bank and the International Monetary Fund set up after World War II) and the World Trade Organization (WTO). These old structures, including the United Nations, were and often still are seen as large, reactive, rigid and slow. They have played their role well in the past, but at present seem left behind with the pace of change. New players, such as the World Economic Forum, the G8, non-governmental organizations

FIGURE 6.1 Headquarters locations of Forbes top 2,000 firms

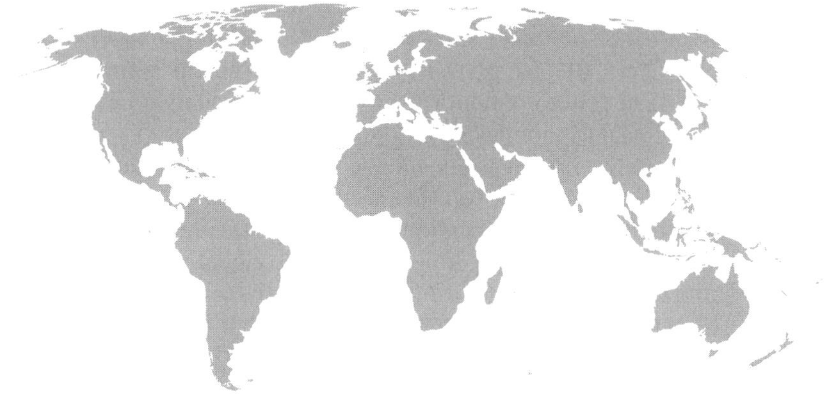

Regions	No. HQs
Africa	34
Central & South Asia	58
Eastern Europe	50
Middle East	59
North America	638
Pacific Rim	631
South America	52
Western Europe	485

Pacific					
Australia	46	Japan	270	South Korea	51
China	162	Malaysia	18	Taiwan	39
Indonesia	10	Philippines	3	Thailand	14
		Singapore	18		

SOURCE: Forbes[3]

(NGOs) and media, have emerged in the field and shifted power away from the old structures. Newcomers seem to be faster, more proactive, leaner and more flexible.[4]

One beacon corporate exception is Standard Chartered plc, whose whole raison d'être is to build up the business infrastructure of the developing world. And this has transcended into its corporate branding, its corporate mission and values and its corporate people strategy.

But one of the key elements of globalization, if you wish to use the term, is that 'it includes the internationalization of production, a new international division of labour, new migratory movements'.[5]

The new world might be smaller!

The global financial crisis has forced collections of local countries to support their neighbouring currencies to protect their regional economic interests –

understandably, given the depth of the crisis, never experienced before nor its speed of impact.

The reaction of some markets has been to question whether the linkage to a US- or Europe-dominated currency is beneficial in the short or even medium term. This, of course, is tricky in a geopolitical context but in regions where their prime commodity is measured in dollars per barrel, this has become a crucial economic driver.

The main countries driving the economic recovery in the Middle East and Asia are seriously questioning whether they should remain tethered to the US dollar or create their own economic currency zone linked to another, more reliable, benchmark. The prime issue for the global economy today is that oil and gas which will fuel tomorrow's growth are still priced in US dollars. The problem for the emerging markets is that the volatility of the market is so great that they cannot dump the 'greenback' – but the debate is firmly on the agenda.

The Baby Boomer version of the new world is that business and social connections have become smaller as the new world connectivity makes life more immediate, more accessible.

To the global nomad, the opposite applies. Yes, the world has become more accessible but it has just got bigger as more and more countries come in reach for extreme travel – areas once deemed deep and darkest are now sought out as prime locations for adventure. They are even closer physically via connections, via business or charitable works or virtually via the internet or news coverage to become destinations of choice. In their mind a location is only a web link away for a flight, hostel or eco project within the next three months.

A new way of doing business

The key 'nomadic cities' of Dubai, Doha, Singapore, Shanghai, Istanbul, Hyderabad, Kuala Lumpur and Rio de Janeiro are the new gateways into the emerging regions. They are building their reputation on becoming crucial regional hubs. Massive investment in airport and associated land transport infrastructure is geared around moving vast numbers of individuals in transit or ideally for short-term, interval breaks from one destination to another. This true hive of activity and energy is providing the melting pot for nomad interface and exchange.

And corporates are responding accordingly as offices based in these locations are being set up as hubs to serve regional markets as air transportation facilitates linkage to customers and clients without the need to create local market offices, although this remains a key investment call. In the Middle East, for example, the local Gulf Cooperation Council, known as the GCC, is fiercely nationalistic and even 'tribal', expecting or demanding local office presence by city, ie in Jeddah, Riyadh or Abu Dhabi, as well as

Dubai. This again reinforces the importance of face-to-face contact, trust and commitment – e-mail is not enough! These customers and clients expect personal treatment via meetings and telephone calls. Traditional culture is one where an unexpected business visit is treated with enthusiasm and high accommodation rather than high-pressure letters or e-mails requesting response. Once again the emphasis is on the human network – getting to know you personally rather than e-mail, marketing or webinars, a glossy brochure or presentation. For multinationals under cost constraints, this pressure is inflating sales costs. In China, for example, business etiquette requires that the vendor matches the customer in terms of seniority and numbers for any meeting, irrespective of what stage of the beauty parade.

Hence we are seeing that the key to successful business in the emerging markets is all about trust and social networking. In large transformation projects often lasting six to 18 months, the client organization is expecting the supplier to match its in-house team on site. This is a difficult expectation for most professional firms to meet and very hard to refuse. The prevailing Western business model of multinationals fails to flex this reality. UK, German and US day rates (often twice or three times the local rates) cannot match these demands or provide the cross subsidy expected in their stuttering mature markets.

Customers and clients also expect a high degree of flexibility and adaptability:

> Yes, we like the proposed solution but we are unique and will require customization and tailoring to fit our specific needs.
>
> Jordanian bank

This is, of course, a classic negotiating ploy of traders looking to undermine set rules of engagement and pricing models to 'personalize' negotiations to drive a bargain or, in modern parlance, more value.

Emerging market clients also expect an opening gambit to be followed by a request for a 'best price' – these are environments where procurement departments reign supreme. In part this is because many, and in some nations all, firms have direct links to the government or ruling families. Thus the 'private sector' often has classic undertones of governmental bureaucracy and procedure epitomized by contracts and RFPs (requests for proposals).

This creates a real dilemma for multinational corporates under huge pressure to adhere to and implement mature economy regulatory controls but working in countries with less sophisticated regulation and, in some cases, questionable business ethics. Their legal contracts, letters of engagement, codes of conduct are challenged and stretched – sometimes to extremes.

All of which questions whether the business and operating models of the 1970s and 1980s remain valid. Some organizations might claim that these have been updated or evolved but the core assumptions have not changed. Yet the multinationals still persist in these definitions on the grounds that getting it right in the home markets is what matters and the emerging markets are the cream to top the trifle rather than the core recipe. Arguably this is being turned upside down.

So, contrary to the idea that the world is bigger as a result of globalization, I suggest that the immediate future may be one of regionalization. In fact, some people might claim that virtualization will dominate in 2020 whereby face-to-face transactions will be replaced by video conferencing or web-based interactions by actors or even avatars. This is a scary prospect and given the deep cultural instincts of the developing nations is hopefully flawed. However, the concept that the world has become an increasingly bigger place to do business in is undeniable.

The issues are not just a problem for traditional multinational organizations. National incumbents, typically in telecommunications, utilities or energy sectors, which have been privatized, have been forced to seek growth abroad as their home markets are opened up for competition.

In the pre-Lehman boom years, these semi-governmental organizations (often with national golden shares) used rising oil and gas revenues to acquire similar entities in nearby countries. Qatar Telecom and Etislat (the United Arab Emirates telecom provider) have bought over 20 subsidiaries in the course of 24 months. The goal for many of these organizations was not 'globalization' but to become regional players and then to use this strength to expand elsewhere.

Of interest, many have mission statements which declare the aim of becoming a top-10 or -20 global organization but not to be *the* global player. Unlike the top multinationals who promised shareholders global domination and growth, these local organizations have set out a growth strategy within regional markets where 'wider local market' knowledge in language, consumer behaviour and expectations can be leveraged against multinational firms. Campaigns and brands are specifically targeted to local customs and timetables.

How many multinational executives know of, or understand, the Islamic Hijri calendar and the importance of the moon and Ramadan or the Indian festivals of Diwali or the significance of the Chinese New Year? You need to be there and live there to appreciate how important these events are to the people and their businesses. In the past few years as these markets grew, many multinationals responded by saying these are 'opportunities', looking to fly in specialists and key professionals as required but remaining focused on core Western, English-speaking markets where they know what they are dealing with, have similar legal entities and acknowledged business protocols.

But the tide has turned. As Philip Stevens, writing in the *Financial Times* on 15 October 2009, stated:

> As the financial crash fades in the memory, the world's rising economies are not about to take any more lectures from the West on the virtues of liberal markets ... what will interest them [historians] is not a change in

the nature of capitalism but the shift in the distribution of global economic power. The market no longer belongs to the West.

'Opportunist' business activity does not work in these markets given the need to build relationships over a period of time. Customers are expecting hands-on, site-based commitment and a proven record of deliverables. To this end, local organizations often test their business partners by significant delays in meetings, postponements, rescheduling, altered scope and changed agendas. Some Western firms find this behaviour to be frustrating or unprofessional but this is how Eastern trade is conducted, with more ebb and flow. The answer is to go with the flow.

Another feature of organizations in emerging markets is that they are often consensual in both governance and decision making. This can mean that commercial decisions are unlikely to be finalized in an initial meeting, where the objective is more about getting to know each other as possible partners. Recommendations are likely to run through several iterations before being finalized and might not even be adopted. Hence a key competence for organizations in the new world will be to deploy senior executives to build relationships based on trust and networks. This plays well to the idea of 'born-again' nomadic Boomers in the twilight of their professional careers.

As larger organizations in these markets are often new (most less than 20 years old), some of their functions – notably HR but you can easily add finance, marketing, customer service to the list – are nascent, with little more than administrative processes. These processes are often manual rather than computerized and few have fully integrated ERP (enterprise resource planning) facilities. Given many have been spawned out of former government entities (and may still have dominant government shareholding) there is a tendency towards bureaucratic paperwork and legality. Finalizing contracts might actually occur post-event and often will require clarification or modification of terms. Match this with the agility of start-ups, often unregulated firms, and the building of web-based internet lookalikes, and a further degree of unpredictability is added. So another required competence is risk assessment, combined with courage, to run with certain projects but be able to reject others even if the promised returns seem enticing.

The emerging markets are learning fast. They have not had to go through centuries of development and have been able to latch onto new technologies, for example cellular and wireless telephony. Rather than investing in outdated infrastructure, desalination for irrigation, advanced geophotography to spot mining deposits, they have been able to leapfrog their economic development. They are also acting together, replicating the trading blocs of the European Union through Asean (Association of South-eastern Nations), GCC (the Gulf Co-operation Council), NAFTA/Cono Sur (South America). Combined with their new-found strength coming out of the financial crises, this puts a major onus on multiculturalism. They have already invested in learning two or three business languages, whilst some

Western firms have rested on the laurels of English language dominance, assuming everyone will come around to their systems and their way of doing things. This arrogance, reflected in both commercial and political actions in the past 10 years, is now openly challenged. The time is ripe for a new set of business norms and ethics which are more universal.

With increasing regulation and investor pressure, major corporates have had to place greater emphasis on improved business ethics, governance and corporate responsibility. For example, Goldman Sachs, enjoying a solid revival from the crash, is under huge public pressure to match its profits and proposed bonus payments with substantial charitable donations. Now many major corporates in both the mature and emerging markets have created foundations to channel money and expertise to good causes in the developing world.

As a result the new world organizations are reviewing their mission, vision and values statements. Whilst they want best practices as benchmarks, these remain more directional, as what they really want is to implement best fit for their organizations.

The mission statements have become more responsive to both sensitivities and their responsibilities in their new markets. See Figure 6.2.

FIGURE 6.2 Mission statements

Our mission is to add vitality to life. We meet everyday needs for nutrition, hygiene and personal care with brands that help people look good, feel good and get more out of life.

We discover new medicines that are designed to improve the health and quality of life of patients around the world.

Attain leadership through business excellence in the sectors we operate in, while upholding our values and integrity, to improve the quality of life of the communities we serve.

Our principles: Leading by example to be the right partner for its stakeholders, the group is committed to building a sustainable business over the long term that is trusted worldwide for upholding high standards of corporate governance, social responsibility, environmental protection and employee diversity.
What we stand for: strategic intent: to be the world's best international bank; leading the way in Asia, Africa and the Middle East.

To focus on our customers' market challenges and needs by providing excellent communications network solutions and services in order to consistently create maximum value for customers (with a) vision to enrich life through communication.

FIGURE 6.2 continued

ThyssenKrupp

As one of the world's leading technology enterprises, ThyssenKrupp has a particular responsibility for the people directly and indirectly affected by our work. This responsibility is reflected in our wide-ranging activities to support people and the environment. It is one of our chief priorities to take into account business, social and ecological aspects in our decisions. ThyssenKrupp … has a long and successful tradition of corporate responsibility. As well as taking responsibility for what goes on in our subsidiaries, we also make an active contribution to solving social problems and foster the positive development of the regions in which we operate. To this end we support a number of non-profit projects, organizations and initiatives in culture, science, education and sport as well as other social, charitable and humanitarian activities.

RioTinto

Rio Tinto's vision is to be the global mining leader. Our vision shapes our core objective, which is to maximize total shareholder return by sustainably finding, developing, mining and processing natural resources. Rio Tinto's reputation for acting responsibly plays a critical role in our success as a business and our ability to generate shareholder value. Our reputation stems from our four core values, which define the essence of who we are and who we will be: accountability, respect, teamwork and integrity.

Nestlé is committed to the following business principles in all countries, taking into account local legislation, cultural and religious practices: Nestlé's business objective is to manufacture and market the company's products in such a way as to create value that can be sustained over the long term for shareholders, employees, consumers, and business partners.
Nestlé does not favor short-term profit at the expense of successful long-term business development.
Nestlé recognizes that its consumers have a sincere and legitimate interest in the behavior, beliefs and actions of the company behind brands in which they place their trust and that without its consumers the company would not exist.

But most interesting is the fact that the values more strongly reflect the global, multicultural aspects of working environments, in particular stressing respect for others. See Figure 6.3.

FIGURE 6.3 Values

Our corporate purpose states that to succeed requires 'the highest standards of corporate behaviour towards everyone we work with, the communities we touch, and the environment on which we have an impact'.

Integrity and high ethical standards; respect for the individual and diversity; openness, honesty, trust and support for each other; leadership by examples at all levels.

Our values: courageous; responsiveness; international; creative; trustworthy; commitment to stakeholders.
Customers: passionate about our customers' success, delighting them with the quality of our service.
Our people: helping our people to grow, enabling individuals to make a difference and teams to win.
Communities: trusted and caring, dedicated to making a difference.
Investors: a distinctive investment delivering outstanding performance and superior returns.
Regulators: exemplary governance and ethics wherever we are.

At Mars, our five principles (quality, responsibility, mutuality, efficiency and freedom) guide us in the daily choices we make and the manner in which we do business. Two in particular stand out. For us, 'a mutual benefit is a shared benefit: a shared benefit will endure' and responsibility states that 'as individuals we demand total responsibility from ourselves'. Mutuality and responsibility impose a special obligation upon us. We take upon ourselves the responsibility for seeking to ensure that we deliver mutual benefit to all with whom we interact: associates, consumers, trade partners, our communities, and last but not least our planet. Our actions should never be at the expense, economic or otherwise, of others with whom we work. We strongly believe that only success that is shared can be sustained and it is our goal to achieve this in all we do.

FIGURE 6.3 continued

Tata has always been values driven. These values continue to direct the growth and business of Tata companies. The five core Tata values underpinning the way we do business are:

Integrity: we must conduct our business fairly, with honesty and transparency. Everything we do must stand the test of public scrutiny.

Understanding: we must be caring, show respect, compassion and humanity for our colleagues and customers around the world, and always work for the benefit of the communities we serve.

Excellence: we must constantly strive to achieve the highest possible standards in our day-to-day work and in the quality of the goods and services we provide.

Unity: we must work cohesively with our colleagues across the group and with our customers and partners around the world, building strong relationships based on tolerance, understanding and mutual cooperation.

Responsibility: we must continue to be responsible, sensitive to the countries, communities and environments in which we work, always ensuring that what comes from the people goes back to the people many times over.

So a major change is that these companies are seeking out new customers from the emerging markets as a set strategy, not simply the opportunism of the past, and in doing so are changing both their brand reputation and their way of doing business.

It is not the emerging market firms who are coming under scrutiny in respect of their values, but the multinationals, who are under the spotlight. Organizations need to check that their employment brand not only resonates to the outside world, especially new graduates, but also to the rising stars of the global nomad world.

But there is another fact; their workforces are changing too.

References

1 World Bank (2000) 'Poverty in an age of globalization', October, p 1
2 Greenpeace International (2001) 'Safe trade in the 21st century', October, p 23

3 Forbes (2010) 'The world's leading companies – Headquarters Inc.', May, pp 96–7, **www.forbes.com**
4 Carlos Lopes (2000) 'Managing the globalization process – role of United Nations', *UN Chronicle*, Winter
5 Robert Cox (1994) 'Multilateralism and the democratization of world order', paper for the International Symposium on Sources of Innovation in Multilateralism, Lausanne, May 26–28, 1994, cited by J A Scholte in *The Globalization of World Politics* by J Baylis and S Smith (eds), New York: Oxford University Press

The new globally mobile workforce

07

In the past three years, the number of globally mobile employees has trebled to approximately 20 million. Mercer's surveys[1] over the past few years have identified this marked trend as firms are now expecting employees to commit to both short-term and long-term assignments as a direct impact of targeting and winning business in the emerging markets.

Part of this has been driven by more project-based work for a wider range of professional firms whereby work is no longer fully contracted to a multinational but increasingly to a partnering contract with a local organization or as part of a wider consortium of firms to deliver bigger, more ambitious infrastructure projects. A further trend has been greater segmentation of specialist skills by niche firms so that the once all-encompassing conglomerates are now exposed as adopting broad, unbending methodologies, processes or systems competing against best-in-class, agile, adaptable and innovative newcomers. These trends have started to carve out mega projects which might have demanded significant resource teams to be based on site for considerable lengths of time (with even local offices) to a more flexible resourcing model combining global specialists plus local delivery and customer liaison teams.

As competition has grown for business in the emerging markets and potential profit margins have shrunk, so it becomes harder to justify permanent deployment of expat experts to a given country market. It has become more attractive to use such resources on a regional basis, operating out of key hubs to win and support local market business development.

This flexible resourcing (often born out of business necessity rather than design) has meant multinationals are now deploying a multilayered, expatriate model featuring combinations of:

- Commuting senior regional management, whereby regional heads of business are having to spend a set number of days or up to 10–14 days in rotation in key markets.
- Global industry experts are being asked to fly in to address deal-securing technical expertise and regular advisory services to larger regional clients where exposure to the board executives is a necessity.
- Senior strategic expats on medium-term contracts are expected to build up local market development, establishing and maintaining key account relationships with highly influential local business and political leaders.
- Medium-term corporate seconded seasoned professionals as trusted professional advisers and project managers for the duration of specific projects or a number of similar projects whilst the market need is apparent.
- Locally contracted expats with proven technical methodology or professional skills brought in to act as local delivery teams with local national professionals to fast-track delivery against agreed proposals.
- Local professionals and support teams largely to address operational logistics, local language interfaces with customer/client junior professional and middle management grades.

The problem is that many of these pioneering outposts have been staffed up by ambitious Generation X and/or Y folk whose appetite for adventure and the chance of rapid career advancement does not match up to the 'globally loaded' professional rates or seniority expectations of the customers. In seeking best-practice professional advice to be ahead of the market, these companies are expecting presentation *and* delivery from the supplier's top team. The latter is particularly problematic for many professional firms as their Western-based leveraged resourcing models are based on partners or principals developing and winning business, with the majority of work completed by supporting teams of mid- to lower-level professionals.

In the emerging markets, the expat professional is often considered as a hired hand to be on site and available at any beck and call. And this is likely to be outside normal working hours for the senior staff. It is partly because the local business leadership in these markets is often concentrated in the hands of relatively few individuals who are spread thinly through their multiple business interests (often as sponsors – and hence board members – to a number of enterprises they have spawned). Board meetings in the Middle East, for example, are often held late into the evening. Coupled with variances in accepted weekends – Thursday–Friday in Saudi Arabia or Friday–Saturday in other Middle East states – this places huge burdens on the regional senior management, the global fly-in experts and regional experts (ie multinationals' most senior staff) who not only have to cope with these immediate customer/client expectations but also juggle their work–life balance given that the rest of the world (and in particular, their Western corporate masters) is still working on a different week, let alone time zones. Somehow US multinationals (since the majority are US-owned) still do not understand that setting conference calls for midday on a Friday (or actually any day) is either the weekend or midnight in the Middle or Far East. Yet this is where an increasingly significant amount of their business is being done. The reality is, of course, complete breakdown of any semblance of work–life balance, with most of these folk working a six- or seven-day week, often of 80 to 90 hours on a regular basis. Coupled with rising air travel as a result of the expansion and explosion of these markets, requiring journeys on regular if not a daily basis across one or more time zones, the physical and psychological burden is huge.

In the past, expats were prepared to pack up their bags and move because these appointments came with generous packages, lifestyles and corporate career advancement which could be contemplated for a relatively short assignment period. However, as the multinationals have progressively reduced this advantage along with governments clawing back tax regimes, the concept of betterment has been replaced with one of package equalization through the widely adopted 'balance sheet' approach for expatriate remuneration. Whilst in practice there is some advantage, this is quickly eroded through the general hassle factor, often generated or sponsored by the multinational employer.

A pressing need to adopt more flexible workforce practices

So the multinational firms are facing a growing dilemma – they want and need an increasingly flexible, global workforce but on consistent standard terms and conditions, even though the logistics of different country tax regimes, significant variances in cost of living indices, currency fluctuations, educational and medical arrangements mean a 'one size fits all' policy is flawed.

And not surprisingly the reaction from this rising nomadic workforce is a demand for more flexibility, more personal choice, understanding and tolerance of the working realities. Generation Y, remember, is quite prepared to adapt and meet unexpected business challenges but only as long as the burdens and efforts beyond contractual duty are recognized, acknowledged and compensated. Given the unpredictability of business in emerging markets, multinationals will be well advised not to take their general acceptance of demands beyond the norm for granted. This group are very driven – their desire to delight the customer/client is probably higher than that of any previous generation, in part through their intellectual drive for excellence. The psychological contract, if there ever was one, is extremely fragile and is not shown as the whingeing grievance typical of frustrated Baby Boomers or the moody Generation X but by a real 'get up and go' attitude through the corporate door.

First this means that the multinationals will need to introduce more diverse workforce practices to cater and compensate for this increasingly diverse global workforce. As recent reports suggest that one quarter of the world's population is Muslim and predominately located in the Eastern emerging markets, this will require the multinationals to accommodate key tenets of the faith – which is more than a religion but a series of guidances for daily life. Hence this will require significant corporate understanding and respect to individual dress, working time (including prayer time), national and religious holidays.

But rather than agonize about the construct or wording of diversity policies, firms would be best advised to hear out comment from employees themselves. So often the problem of such initiatives stems from corporate-inspired committees led by inappropriately appointed managers who feel they must establish principles and policy statements without involving and gleaning opinions from the very employees affected.

The good news is that the new workforce will not be shy in giving feedback. Second, rather than setting out a series of 'unproductive' demands reminiscent of former trade union bargaining, the overall result is likely to be highly accommodating from a group respecting many cultures and with an inherent global mindset.

Addressing the social networking issue

Today the end user has many new forms of communication based around social networks: in addition to e-mail there are now collaborative websites, wikis, podcasts, 'mash-ups' (integrating content from more than one source) and blogs, which allow individuals opportunities in how to mix content. YouTube was founded in February 2005 and is the world's most popular online video community. People are watching 2 billion videos a day on YouTube and uploading hundreds of videos daily. In fact, every minute 24 hours of video is uploaded to YouTube.[2] Given that Generation Y want to be online and connected at all times, firms are beginning to look at social networking as a new business model that can be leveraged for marketing, building brand loyalty, customer care and recruiting. This new form of connecting allows people to connect based on common and shared interests, and provides a unique opportunity for companies to tap into this new model to increase productivity and tap into other forms of reaching employees, partners and customers as well as new customers and markets.

This social structure of individuals, business partners, friends and organizations is allowing connectivity via a range of technology using all sorts of devices (PCs, cellphones, PDAs, digital TVs, etc). This new collaboration is being generated and pushed to people and businesses by end users. One of our case studies features Cisco, which is at the heart of this new human network – the fabric that ties it all together.

Recent research from Flowtown[3] shows that 79 per cent of the Fortune 100 companies are using at least one of the following: Facebook, Twitter, YouTube or flow-fortune. But noticeably the proportion of European firms using all the major sites is less than half that of the USA or Asia, whilst the emerging countries are significantly ahead in broader adoption. A message here, methinks.

Multinationals have reacted to social network sites such as Facebook or Twitter in mixed fashion. Research by Nicholas Oxley states that whilst many organizations have utilized the internet for recruitment via corporate websites or commercial job-board sites, 'the general approach of employers has remained the same ... and in reality the internet has enabled the transfer of traditional recruitment methods to the web. Certainly it improved the reach and efficiency of recruitment, but the richness of these activities did not greatly improve'.[4]

For Generation Y the internet has become an indispensable tool for communication, information and collaboration. The issue of social networking is that it presents today's employers with increased scrutiny of their corporate communications and activities; it has also blurred the boundary between home and work and its also requires continual innovation. Some professional social networks like LinkedIn are also experiencing massive growth in membership. The difficulty is that these sites allow information to be circulated in real time across the internet without control. This can harm organizations' integrity and reputations.[5] Some organizations have also raised concern that employee productivity is affected and they have responded by banning use of social networking sites in the office. This will irk the new generational workforce.

The global nomads are at the sharp end of this trend; their physical distance from family and friends has meant social networking is key to staying connected. Multinational firms would do better to review how staff use these sites rather than ban them. As our case study of News Corp illustrates (see Chapter 14), companies can proactively engage the use of these sites or their own variant to channel energy, communication and recommendations for innovation. The case study of Cisco Systems (see Chapter 14) takes this further and now has created a new organization design based on who is linked to whom rather than a hierarchical structure typically based on tenure, experience and what people know.

Reviewing traditional organizational structures

All of the above is also beginning to question whether traditional models of organization structure are so relevant in the new normal. For the past 25 years, most major firms have adopted one or other typical organization structure: functional or geographical. The functional model is based on expertise in set disciplines and clear business process to underpin corporate strategies – typically a series of operational divisions mandated to produce or deliver specific customer products or service lines to match market needs. An indicative structure is shown in Figure 7.1.

The accountabilities of these functions depend on developing standardized product and services at least cost so that profit can be leveraged from replication and assurance of quality.

By focusing on process and delivery mechanisms, the corporate multinational proposition is one of 'guaranteeing' the same level of service to consumers anywhere in the world whether this be a McDonald's quarter pounder, a Pantene shampoo or a bottle of Coke. Hence the power of the global brand is to unite consumers around an expectation of what will be delivered and an ability to shut out local competitors or suppliers of alternative products.

The functional model also concentrates strategy and key decision making in a small number of supporting functions, notably corporate strategy, finance, IT, marketing and human resources (HR). Here the driver, in theory, is to ensure corporate systems and corporate thinking are uniform, with set reporting mechanisms to facilitate collation and consolidation of data to allow more robust, rapid decision making at the centre.

In the past, multinational firms looked on the developing world as a source of materials and labour to subsidize the rising cost of production and delivery in their all-important home markets given rising standards of living and hence the rising disposable income of the population. Certain functions are becoming more global simply because of trading necessities – supply chain and logistics management is an obvious case in point.

And the same applies in the world of professional services, if not more so. The major accounting firms, banks and consulting firms all look to present themselves as global players able to satisfy major corporates' needs across the globe to specific methodologies and specific standards (many of which are set internally). But as much of the growth of this business has come through acquisitions of local firms into the corporate giant, each acquisition has brought a slightly different heritage, new management and often a new niche methodology and perspective. In some cases these firms look more like federations or collections of partnerships rather than unified, homogenous operating units.

Thus over the past five to 10 years, partly as a result of the significant growth in acquisitions, many multinationals have embarked on major initiatives to drive a unified 'one way' with the prime objectives of simplification, common methodology and a customer promise of consistency.

But the Western image of global commercialization has gone hand in hand with a tarnishing of political policy plus weakening of market strength as local and regional companies start to tailor more closely to local needs. As a result more and more variations and changes in product look, taste, feel, and smell have appeared.

FIGURE 7.1 Functional organization structure

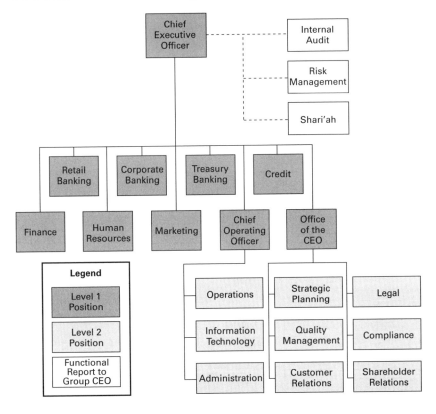

The second major organizational design option is geographical. This primarily acknowledges that with the growing world of trade where the lines of delivery and communication have become so stretched, it becomes important to establish local centres, not just representative offices. Firms have also realized that using local production and service delivery could also provide specific advantage in using local knowledge to maximize sales, reduced cost of assembly and production plus enhanced reputation as a provider of local employment. The major problem of the geographical model is that local units have a tendency to mimic the mother ship and want to establish their own support functions, notably finance, HR, IT, marketing, etc, which then dilutes the efficiency of the corporate centre. See Figure 7.2.

Hence the dilemma: on one hand, centralized functional structures fail to allow for market variation and requirements whilst on the other, geographical structures tend to replicate corporate structures and hence lose synergy and add more cost. This is the fundamental conflict between global versus local and has prompted a whole host of hybrid alternatives to create 'glocal' structures, all with mixed success.

FIGURE 7.2 Geographical organization structure

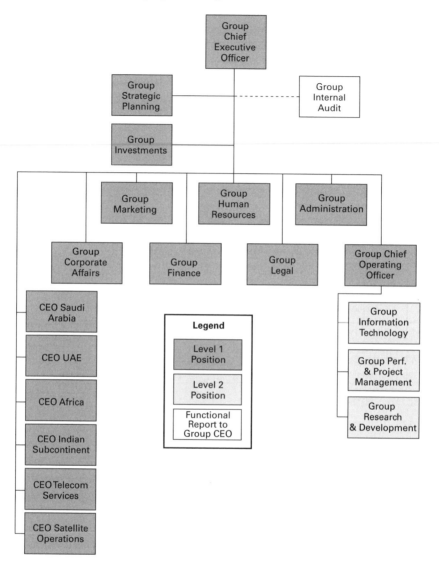

The attraction is to create a 'matrix structure' which combines the best of both the functional and geographical models. Such models are hard to implement, mainly because they are usually replacing one of the traditional models. Hence there will be trade-offs and a power shift one way or the other, and therefore they carry risks.

Once multinationals reach a certain size, complications can set in. When you have over 10,000 employees operating in over 100 locations in 20-plus countries there is a difficulty that country-based operations with full profit and loss (P&L) accountability fail to create the critical mass to penetrate local markets sufficiently and typically duplicate overheads. But of greater concern is that core offerings are often delivered with local interpretations, leading to inconsistent delivery and, most notably, pricing variation between regions. Whilst this might reflect the realities of local P&Ls, they are all too obvious to major global customers. Some, therefore, have moved to the 'super-geography' model based loosely on the continents – Americas, Europe, Middle East and Africa (EMEA) and Asia-Pacific. On paper, this would seem to make sense given time zones and travel commitments, but in practice the model fails to recognize that Europe is a collection of 25-plus countries, each with different legal jurisdictions and languages. It is even worse in Asia-Pacific, where there are five time zones covering 48 countries with 80 languages, 27 religions and 37 different currencies. In China there may be one written alphabet but there are eight separate dialects, which means that a native Chinese in one area might not understand others in another region.

In matrix structures, multinationals typically try to organize to be client or customer centred with lines of businesses providing world-class solutions (combining products and services) but with global marketing taking care of brand, integrating service delivery and a focus on strategic, global account relationships (those clients or customers operating in all three super-geographies.) The super-geographies remain responsible for presenting the company with the one face transcending business and local country boundaries. Internal functions are charged with streamlining and globalizing core processes to drive efficiency, consistency and quality.

In the professional services sector, the logic is that such a combination of structures working in unison provides the following benefits:

- An opportunity to bring global solutions to clients with better consistency and coordination, so clients receive the best from the firm.
- Allows organizations to innovate more quickly, so clients get cutting-edge advice.
- Streamline internal processes by reducing barriers to get the organization's best people in front of clients, giving an access to a wealth of intellectual capital and global services.
- Provide more added value by combining global and local expertise, perspectives and solutions.
- Establish a greater focus on the largest multinational clients, to ensure the firm brings the best services, resources and solutions to the table.

Whilst internally providing:

- More interesting career paths and professional growth opportunities.

- Reducing internal barriers to providing seamless client-focused work by speeding up decision making and execution.
- Allowing employees working in such an global entity more opportunities for more people to participate in global projects.
- Creating a collaborative work environment where people find their work stimulating and rewarding, supported by better tools and global processes that save time and improve the quality of work.

The theory sounds terrific and the example below illustrates this notion of organization design. It seeks to enhance customer relationships by focusing effort on key clients by moving from managing projects to managing client accounts and relationships to focus effort on resolving client business issues and providing added-value insight rather than delivering reactive, transactional services. In doing so, the organization believed it would drive business growth by growing account revenue through proactive and coordinated teamwork with the sector knowledge providing the necessary insights, direction and strategy. It aimed to clarify accountability between geographies, sectors and consulting specialities.

However its implementation hit problems as the various business leaders were unable to agree on the purpose, mandates and performance expectations of decision-making bodies, appropriate spans of control and the new reporting lines. Rather than simplifying the organization, the matrix actually increased management hierarchy as many tough decisions were fudged given the personalities involved.

FIGURE 7.3 Matrix organization structure

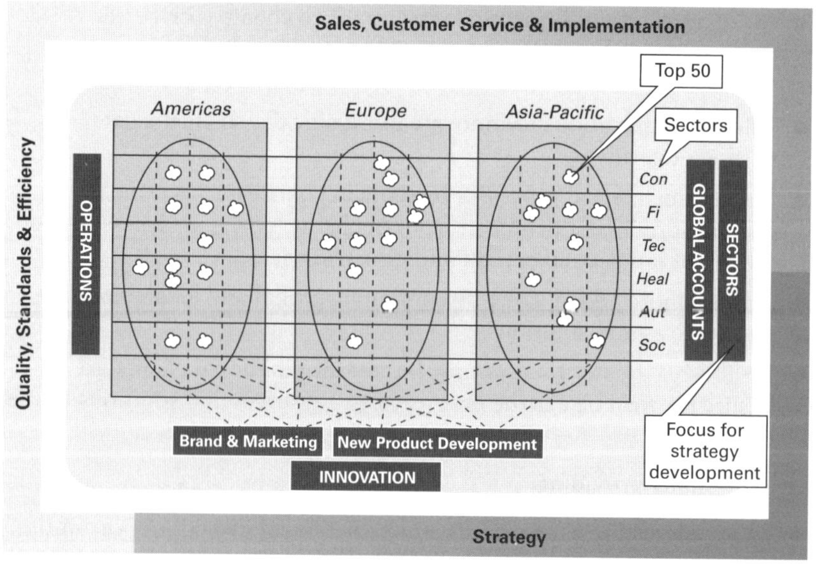

The matrix is tricky to implement mainly because of traditional political structures where functions or geographies are not prepared to give up their controlling decision making to the new 'coordinating' bodies – in particular strategy to new global sales and marketing groups or global finance. Often the success of local units has come from their agility to meet local market needs through 'customization', flexibility on pricing and labour costing.

Local units are particularly sensitive in respect of sales and marketing control. There is always an argument that a particular country or region is 'different', that business is conducted in a 'different manner' and has particular cultural sensitivities. The predominately US or Western corporates have found these variations difficult to swallow and frustrating to a machine looking to generate replicable product or service consistency throughout the globe. Ironically these structural changes and their ramifications are nearly always internally focused in debate, creating huge amounts of angst, confusion and destabilization whilst clients and customers (the intended beneficiaries of these changes) either are oblivious of the change or are quite frankly not interested in how organizations want to organize themselves. In the example shown in Figure 7.3, the organization was so keen to communicate the new philosophy and structure it ran a series of road shows externally to its clients and was surprised to hear back: 'It sounds great, so when do we meet our new global team and experience these new benefits?' Shame that the senior management and marketing teams had forgotten to take their employees on the same journey!

But in the new normal world economy, are global consistency, standards and process what regional customers or clients actually want? Undoubtedly for most multinationals, the relatively small number of truly global clients or customers are looking for consistency in standards, quality of product and service. Much of this philosophy was, of course, based around Pareto theory, which implies that for many multinationals 80 per cent of their total revenue is derived from some 20 per cent of their clients or customers. But increasingly these global customers are also expecting their partners and suppliers to pass on price reductions as organizations look to outsource or relocate their production centres in lower-labour-cost countries. So these margins are being squeezed. Thus the true value of the 20 per cent is shrinking.

Often the multinationals have a long tail of locally based clients and customers which have often been 'over-served' by local units given their low revenue stream and profitability. As these emerging markets develop and change more rapidly than ever before, many of these local clients and customers are now aspiring to be serious regional players. However, coming from a different cultural heritage and with the opportunity of oversight of the shifting economic fortunes, many of these organizations are not setting their sights on becoming global giants but are looking for measured growth market by market in neighbouring countries partly because they have more in common and hence know these markets better and partly because they are cautious in acquiring competitors in distant lands where language, culture and customer taste are significantly different. The Asian conglomerates of Korea (known as Chaebol) and Japan have traditional, strong family-centred cultures with credos to match, which mirror their societies at large. Their forays into the Western markets have had painfully chequered histories as they met with consumer prejudice, workforce misunderstanding and resistance to change. As the recovery takes hold in these Eastern markets, Western multinationals would do well to reflect on the Arabic notion of '*al ehtiram*' or more widely '*etiram al aadat*' (broadly translated as 'respect' or 'respect of cultural traditions'). Rather than criticizing their national traits and culture, this essentially says 'We have invited you to our house; you should show more respect in how we go about our lives.' This is equally true in business.

With the shift in economic markets, firms in these countries are less impressed with the multinationals' 'global' credentials as the talent and skill gap in expertise is rapidly evaporating whilst at the same time local markets are looking to firms to meet local styles, tastes and sensitivities. The new power brokers in the Middle East, Asia and Latin America are flexing their muscles to expect more local delivery, greater customization to their specific needs and greater personal investment in time and energy. The Western leveraged model of resourcing based around concentrated research into home market consumerism or professional needs which created predominately US and European intellectual capital is being challenged.

With the emerging markets no longer 'opportunist' but actually key or even the major contributors of current and future corporate revenue, it is time to review the underlying business models, organization structures, management culture and performance and reward systems. These need more flexibility to allow variation by region to match the ever-increasing mix of people, culture and their societies. The 'one size fits all', cookie-cutter management school theories of the 1990s might not be so appropriate.

References

1 Mercer (2009) 'Worldwide benefits and employment guidelines', July
2 www.youtube.com/t/fact_sheet, 11 November 2010
3 'How are companies leveraging social media?' Ethan Bloch, **www.flowtown.com**, 7 March 2010
4 'Social Media Recruitment – A Danger to Ignore?', dissertation presented by Nicholas Oxley, University of Edinburgh, 2009.
5 **www.youtube.com/watch?v=xaNuE3DsJHM**

PART FOUR
Building a new management framework

Introduction

So how are multinationals responding? Many now accept that change must happen to seize the new opportunities in the so-called 'new normal'. For many, increasing regulation, government intervention through rising nationalization, tightening fiscal and labour market laws have forced a re-evaluation of business and organization models plus realignment of their workforces. The big change here has been a huge focus on evidence-based data to support future investments.

Restructuring is now being replaced by fact-based workforce planning – not just in terms of headcount but also in terms of capability, ie skills, competencies and productivity. There is a dominant theme of looking to upskill existing resources. This is also coupled with a shift in leadership and commercial competencies with more emphasis on relationship building, multicultural awareness and strategy execution. What is happening is that Asian and Middle Eastern models are emerging to replace the traditional US-centric frameworks.

In addition, firms need to manage the workforce – especially their global nomads – in a new way. Most significantly, the multinationals need to tune into their workforce's energy to inspire passion, commitment and loyalty in their changing workforce. This will require a new employment proposition, particularly for those key individuals who will spearhead tomorrow's growth. As all these factors are interrelated and interdependent, a new holistic management framework is required.

Adjusting for change

08

The lack of confidence, collapse of credit and non-commitment meant that a good number of firms which had been gearing up for continued growth suddenly found their revenue streams drying up and their overall profit forecasts rapidly evaporating. Many decided to sit out the pain for the first two quarters of 2009 but took the knife to overheads in the next two quarters. As we have seen before, the financial crisis has actually spurred managements on to take the hard decisions which had been delayed and fudged in previous years when growth had allowed organizations to carry a number of passengers. In previous recessions in the 1980s and 1990s, companies in the mature markets typically applied blanket cuts across all departments, which had unequal impact. For example, taking a 10 per cent cut across the board was an easy 'democratic' decision but meant smaller or recently created functions felt the pain disproportionately. This particularly impacted areas of innovation, for example research and development, brand marketing and product management, which were typically embryonic, gearing up for future growth. This seriously impacted organizations' ability to take advantage of any upturn and in some cases damaged efficiency and shareholder value.

In the early 1990s, I was consulting to a number of police forces in the UK who were faced with such a demand from central government. One constabulary withdrew 10 per cent of its police cars on such a basis, which made little sense given it was a rural force, whilst another applied some lateral thinking to replace its cars with motorcycles given it was an urban force where bikes were more effective in weaving in and out of traffic and so getting to crime scenes more quickly.

Another dinosaur of that decade was the trade union philosophy of 'first in, last out'. Clearly understandable from a union perspective of protecting loyal members who had been paying years of subscriptions, it actually led to major labour imbalances in certain industries, notably in the utility sector where many firms had moved from the public sector to the private sector.

After years of gradual restructuring, this practice created an ageing workforce whereby all the feeder recruitment (typically graduate professional intake) was cut out, leaving only the most senior skilled technicians in the company. One such energy firm woke up when its pension manager highlighted an operational cliff that 67 per cent of the organization would retire in the next seven years. Given the current cutback in graduate recruitment over the past 18 months, history might be about to repeat itself. This lack of effective workforce planning in most companies is now highlighting similar issues in many sectors such as oil, electricity, water, aerospace, nuclear energy, rail transport, heavy manufacturing and the automobile industry.

The rise of talent management techniques has allowed companies to apply more targeted, selective culls. In present times, with the absence of workforce planning in place, organizations are asking how to reassess their workforces in the short term. In essence this comes down to two key analyses – the need to identify critical roles and critical people.

Critical positions are those mission critical, strategic or operational roles which if left unfilled for six to nine months will seriously impact the future direction of the company – typically directors or heads of product development, corporate strategy, finance, marketing, IT – or they may be hard-to-fill positions which can affect brand positioning, local market presence or put existing contracts at risk.

Positions which often have critical people or key talents in place also need examination. The danger here is that if these employees leave, they hurt the business significantly. They typically occupy key customer or supplier relationships roles such as key account directors. If these people depart, business will depart with them – usually to a competitor. Key talents also include the high potentials and future leaders which an organization should be grooming for bigger and higher-impact roles. Again, if these people leave, years of sunk training and development will be wasted.

Unfortunately, whilst such analyses are front of mind during growth cycles, in turbulent and volatile times an organization's focus changes and there is a general tendency to home in on perceived core activity. I am witnessing companies becoming inwardly driven with an overbearing obsession to demand reporting on cost and sales. So much so that often the very functions they are urging to secure revenue (new or existing) are so overburdened by reporting demands that they cannot spend sufficient time in the marketplace. Similarly, budgets for marketing and customer service are often the first to be cut in such scenarios, allowing competitors and new entrants to threaten the customer base whilst finance and internal communications often maintain headcount given the perceived importance of their areas to pull the organization through. But hey, this is corporate life!

These periods of turmoil do provide real opportunities for organizations to refresh and develop. This shift in headcount adjustment has also prompted organizations to seek out a 'new structure' and institute reforms long overdue. In the Western economies, many companies have embarked on a

FIGURE 8.1 Tracking career paths

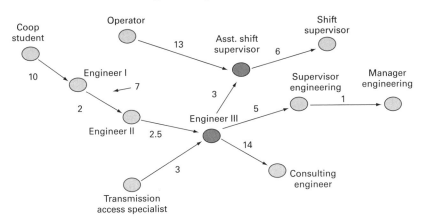

SOURCE: 'Play to Your Strengths' by Haig R Nalbantian, Richard A Guzzo, Dave Kieffer and Jay Doherty[1]

wave of cost cutting and downsizing, in some cases sacrificing sacred taboos of 'no redundancies' and taking the opportunity (out of necessity) of renegotiating labour agreements, as in the US car industry, and reviewing three-year operational strategies.

This has led to what Mercer is describing as 'rightsizing, rightshaping and rightskilling'.

Rightsizing is an appropriate term. For some organizations the recession demanded significant downsizing to address the cost base with the closure of operational sites but for others the next few years are real opportunities for growth, taking advantage of relative weakness of current market incumbents. In certain markets, notably in the Middle East, it is difficult to apply headcount reduction – some countries have issued decrees insisting local nationals cannot be culled even if some organizations have some of these people in their lowest performance rating categories. For these organizations, the issue can be addressed through adjusting the shape of the organization by professionalizing, upskilling the firm and reducing oft-inflated secretarial or office support. The aim is to marginalize the ineffective rump and to encourage a personal choice to seek out new pastures.

The big questions for companies are: What exactly is the right number and how do we get there? Many rush to benchmarking but this is tricky, if not flawed, as an answer. First, there are very few companies which can be compared as 'apples to apples'; even stated peers often turned out to be prickly pears! Furthermore, outside the public sector, few organizations are prepared to share such information for the benefit of a competitor. Benchmarking remains useful from a directional point of

FIGURE 8.2 Rightsizing, rightshaping and rightskilling

- **Rightsizing** – as corporate revenues or income is reduced there is an urgent need to rebalance costs

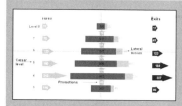

- **Rightshaping** – organizations need to review what core business is and what is not. The harsh economic environment provides an opportunity to re-focus and adjust the shape of the organization

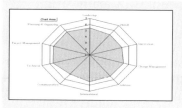

- **Rightskilling** – a chance to re-assess what skills and competencies will be needed to meet the challenge of the recovery and maintain competitive advantage

© Mercer 2009

view, to highlight trends, overall size, broad shape of operations and approach to the market.

Hard data, however, need insight and a playback to a given organization's specific situation (see *Play to Your Strengths*[2]). Typically organizations fall back on some form of activity analysis of the current workforce, often through direct questionnaires to the workforce, but this too will be flawed as the inputs will be heavily biased towards what people do, or think they do, today.

My proposition is to focus on future accountabilities, ie required outcomes as organizations go through transition. The only people who can provide this are the new management who have set out the vision and direction for the firm to follow. Mercer's accountability costing analysis (MACA) does exactly this by mapping a new proposed organization structure to the four or five key accountabilities in each role and the expected time allocation and relative importance of the accountability. Given roles can be costed from a total cash perspective (total employment cost is preferable but hard to do) or a competitive market position for new roles, a strong, robust baseline can be used to evaluate appropriate workforce numbers (steps 1 to 3 in Figure 8.3).

FIGURE 8.3 Mercer's accountability costing analysis

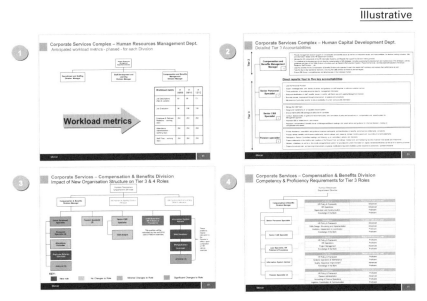

© Mercer 2009

The final step is a question of 'rightskilling'. This takes the proposed organizational roles and identifies the necessary competencies (skills and capabilities) and required proficiency levels. This level of analysis can then prompt the important question of whether the organization needs to buy in (ie recruit) or build (ie develop the existing workforce) based on the business need, the criticality of the role, the availability of the talent internally or in the marketplace.

Another theme is management renewal. Organizations are taking the opportunity of the recession and emerging recovery to freshen up their management teams to prepare for the task ahead for two reasons. First the depth of the crisis has given the chance to reassess the leadership bench strength and the leadership talent pipelines. This is looking to send a clear message to the market, investors and the workforce at large that the organization is shaping up and building anew. The second is a strong message internally to those who have seen out the pain of restructuring that the organization is keen to foster a next wave of talent to flourish in positions often blocked by the 'old school' of the past 10 to 15 years.

Both are now ensuring that new thinking can bubble up and that the vibrant energy of high potentials, so often stifled by the corporation machine, can now be let loose and can inspire the next generation entering the workplace. To do this, however, requires new leadership skills and behaviours which I shall address in the next chapter.

This combination of restructuring, featuring rightsizing, rightshaping and rightskilling, is the opportunity for fundamental review of organization design.

The crisis has provided an opportunity to look to a different, integrated management model. This will need to balance organization development with different ways of working and a new proposition in terms of employee rewards and commitment. In the past many Western organizations have failed to create aligned, integrated people strategies largely because such initiatives were often built off generic best practices but with piecemeal integration without reference to changing business strategies. The growth and pace of the emerging markets are allowing organizations in these regions to consider wholesale transformation of human capital strategies in a set of logical, sequenced interdependent work streams.

An example structure is shown in Figure 8.4. Figure 8.5 expresses this in another way.

FIGURE 8.4 Transforming human capital strategies

1. Management Renewal
2. Top Role Profiles (Tier 1 & 2)
3. Hiring Panel
4. Handwiring / Rightsizing
5. Role Profiling (Tier 3 & 4), Grading & Reward
6. Workforce Planning
7. Performance Management
8. Variable Pay
9. Talent and Succession Management

As we have already discussed, the functional or geographical models for organizations now operating internationally across more than one continent are proving problematic. For the major multinationals, initiating reform with a shift in commercial and decision-making power is hard. Given the shift to new markets, it is surprising to see how many North American multinationals have placed few senior vice presidents and executives who have worked in the new markets or how many of their global leaders are still locally born, with complete under-representation from other regions, irrespective of the contribution of these growing geographies (see Standard Chartered case study in Chapter 14 for the complete opposite).

For European multinationals, the issue is less so, as many of the boards do have a wider, multicultural constitution but even they have a tendency to portray themselves as, for example, German, French or Italian multinationals. This nationalism may in part satisfy local shareholders but it fails to resonate with the emerging markets and the new workforces being built in their various locations further afield.

In the new world, organizations will be judged on their organizational competence (ie competitive strengths and capability), their understanding of

FIGURE 8.5 Work stream sequencing

The sequence is critical because each work stream builds the foundation and inputs for the next module and hence the overall result is a fully integrated plan...

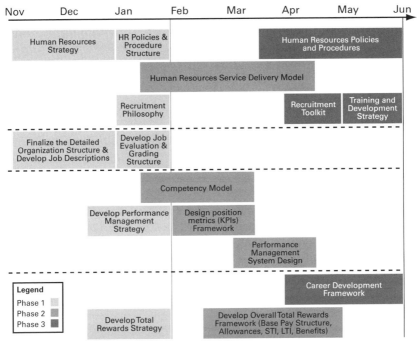

© Mercer 2009

local market needs – and less on their heritage. In a few cases, especially in consumer fashion, there is competitive cachet in stoic national virtues, eg Harrods, Burberry, DKNY, Hilfiger, but in the wider professional services market where project-based business models are emerging, this is not the case. The global nomads have a substantial role in making this 'glocal flexibility' a reality. Some will be the architects and leaders of these new structures; others will be the critical implementers helping to blend strategic and firm-specific expertise with local management and local professionals. These groups will need to work in closer harmony with shared goals, values and ways of working.

Some of my predictions from the previous chapters are:

- The emerging markets are growing in confidence and understand their shaping of future economic trade. For example, in past years many commentators assumed that China was the production room for the world, utilizing its massive available labour to generate cost-efficient, mass-produced products for the mature markets. This has now changed and much of China's recovery centres on its high capital manufacturing base. We know China is producing phenomenal numbers of professionals, especially computer scientists and engineers who need English language and higher technology skills to compete against Western labour but this is a competency gap which is likely to be closed in the next five to seven years.

- The new Asian manufacturing centres will be Vietnam, Cambodia and the Philippines.

- India and Brazil will be the professional powerhouses in the next five years given their investment in education, their growing middle classes and language proficiency skills. This will reflect in prominence in IT, accountancy and professional services. Brazil will continue to grow as an exporter of commodities, especially food but also energy.

- The Middle East, led by the United Arab Emirates, will drive technology-driven innovation given its governmental aspirations, youthfulness as a nation and fascination with high-technology gadgets and the high percentage of under-25s. This will result in continued prominence in industries such as construction and media but these countries will also become centres for biotechnology and energy research (oil, gas, nuclear and renewables).

- The Far East will continue to build on its dominance in nano-technology in terms of computerization, consumer electronics and consumer goods.

These predictions imply far greater segmentation and country or regional specialization. As the emerging markets gain pace in development and their respective offerings to the world, the multinational conglomerates will find their broad portfolio propositions difficult to defend against niche regional players. There will be strong pressure to break up these multidisciplined, multi-product service line giants into more focused leveraged operations. The 'one way cultures' born out of merger and acquisition synergies, cross-selling lines of business and globalization will be challenged by stronger local players.

Global corporate policies, including human resource strategies, which in recent years have focused on 'harmonization', will come under significant strain for more flexibility to reflect local market conditions, different states of emergence, regulatory and business practice. Whilst some might say the world has got smaller and easier to connect it equally can be seen as more diverse in orientation.

Western (US- and European-centric) management models will quickly lose relevance and whilst the best practices will be analysed and dissected, the philosophy for the next five years will become predominately 'best fit', which will mean increasingly demand to customize policy to local or regional markets. The real problem in many international organizations is that the pace of change and transformation of their marketplace is moving faster than their internal organization, in terms of both structure and culture.

So let's look at a slightly different model. It has six foci. Four are at an organizational level and two are targeted at an individual employee level. See Figure 8.6.

FIGURE 8.6 A new management framework

References

1 Haig R Nalbantian, Richard A Guzzo, Dave Kieffer and Jay Doherty (2009) *Play to Your Strengths*, Mercer
2 ibid

Implications for organization design and global leadership

09

T here are two options for change here: one is incremental and simply requires a shift in the balance of power in the matrix; the second is transformational, homing in on the global mobility and generation shift which will occur in the next five to 10 years. In some industry sectors, notably telecoms, media and fashion, this will be faster and so a decision needs to be made now by relevant CEOs; but for most others, the first is probably a halfway house to something different.

Transformational shift

The media sector provides a very good case study. In most companies with regional or global presence what is happening is that the corporation has shifted to become a holding company of brands – News Corporation is a classic example where the consumer is probably unaware of the holding company but instantly resonates with local brands such as Sky, *The Times*, MySpace.com, *The Australian*. However, media organizations are still very silo driven when at the end of the day it is the content which drives consumer traffic and hence revenues. The respective platforms become less important. Why have separate newsrooms for different newspapers, TV, radio and online digital channels? All these journalists, picture editors, video mixers are writing or editing similar stories in 50 per cent of the time yet have their own teams recreating the story and their respective consumer spin.

In today's world, consumers can choose to receive this content in their own way whether this is in a daily national newspaper, via TV or on their mobile phone. This will remain the case in the next five years although there will be an inevitable migration to online delivery, so whilst people might still think it is TV it might not be as we know it today.

This has huge ramifications as internal functional (product line) empires will get cut back but there will be massive efficiency gains and potential added value through the cross-fertilization.

What this example shows is that organizations will need to put their consumers at the centre and organize their delivery operations around them, not some functional, controlling structure based around product or service line. The technology will standardize, so how companies want to organize internally will be of less relevance to end customers; yet today's multinationals still persist with an overriding fascination with separate lines of business P&Ls and key markets.

In the emerging markets, the customer or client also wants more customization, more local delivery, more personalized added value. This requires flexibility, interaction between service lines and a stronger focus on the geographical markets. In this world, the focus is on knowing the customer intimately and understanding customer segment needs. It is about knowing *who* you know and a little less about *what* you know. These new organizations are looking for similar customer/client or industry experience.

Products and services are easily replicated into 'me-too' offerings, so future business will come down increasingly to differentiation in people. And the buying criteria are as simple:

Do I trust this person?

What experience have they got?

Where have they done this before?

Does the chemistry work? (There are horses for courses!)

This is particularly true in the emerging markets, where commercial trading rather than manufacturing has been their traditional mainstay. So if in essence it is about who you know, the professional network becomes critical. This fits well with our new generation workforce who thrive on physical and digital social networking. For them there is no distinction. An option, therefore, is to create a new organization design which might dispense with formal hierarchies and functional reporting lines but instead match key relationships, both external and internal. This would create a commercial version of Facebook, as illustrated in Figure 9.1.

Imagine putting names, role titles, key relationships (external and internal), project experience, key skill sets (eg professional expertise,

FIGURE 9.1 A commercial version of Facebook

industry experience, past and current experience as a pop-up or intelligent search criterion) behind each face and you will have the ability to build customer, event-specific response teams across the world but, most importantly, matching client need first and foremost.

The structure will need to be fluid as project-based work will require permeable teams with a mixture of multidisciplined teams matching customer needs. The structure can be both physical and virtual but what will be required is to leverage knowledge management and technology to the full. Such a structure would be flexible and adaptive and rapidly deployed from regional hubs without the need for the fixed costs of country bases.

This form of structure would suit service-based organizations from technology support, consulting firms or maintenance providers to firms where the customers' products are continually on the move (eg shipping or air transportation).

Incremental change

The incremental alternative implies a shift in the power of matrix organizations with a rebalancing from group functions, notably finance, to customer-facing operations as organizations regain confidence once revenue streams start to show positive trends month on month. But given their headquarters are Western based ie US or Europe based (56 per cent of the top 2,000 multinationals[1]), I anticipate local subsidiaries will start to flex their muscles to take more local control over marketing, sales and customer service. Regionalization will result in more mid-range and multi-country customers. Thus the matrix will morph but with an emerging market orientation rather than a US or similar North American or European bias.

The key to this future model will focus on regional centres such as Dubai/Doha or Kuala Lumpur/Singapore or Hong Kong/Shanghai or Recife/Rio de Janeiro as these cities will own the transportation hubs.

Second, cost constraints will push more and more organizations along the path of outsourcing and operational efficiency. However, as we have seen, some clients and customers will react to this 'low-cost efficiency' model by demanding local country response (eg NatWest's retreat from Indian/Filipino call centres to UK-based operations) to create 'market unique propositions' based on customer feedback about service. This has two outcomes.

First, the low-cost outsourcing model may not be sustainable because the client/customer needs will raise the performance bar, which cannot be matched by standardized responses or a realization that the local service is not quite what it seems. This is a red flag to all multinationals which still have to internalize the switch in emphasis from West to East.

Second, the obvious conclusion is that customers and clients will expect that outsourced operations which are not transparent will deliver the same level of service that they had or expected in their local markets. This will be a huge challenge as it goes to the heart of the traditional, multinational business strategy.

So on both levels, current Western business models may need reworking for the emerging markets. Trying to match customer demand will raise both skill levels and labour cost models. Worse still, seeking out the next low-cost country will also fail because customer expectations are rising faster than most organizations can organize and deploy. In addition, many organizations will have to face the real truth that their 'home market' in the West will no longer be their primary focus as they communicate that the majority of current revenues and future growth will be coming from markets elsewhere.

This will have a significant impact. Most boards in these organizations and their first-line management are still heavily populated by home country incumbents who have 'earned their entitlement' through years of tenure with the company and have been rewarded by career movements which in the main reflected proven local market delivery and loyalty to immediate bosses and their ability to balance home market revenue versus cost reduction centricity. This premise is now being turned upside down by the new normal challenge. (Note that few in the West are using the term 'new world' as this would admit that the shift has already occurred.)

Even worse, I have seen some multinationals react to the 2007 financial crisis in the following way:

> Given the crisis, we must at all costs protect revenue streams in our home markets. Risk management is the name of the game – cut investments anywhere and preserve our established customer market relationships.

Let's regroup with local talent, eliminate risk and rebuild our global proposition based on cost reduction and efficiencies which are leaner and stronger for the new normal so we can withstand future market volatility.

These attitudes have created a perfect opportunity for international competitors in the emerging markets, allowing them to step up in these defining moments of indecision and inertia.

A case example is Abu Dhabi Media Company (ADMC). Two years ago this was a national broadcasting institution of 40 years' heritage, which was trying to preserve Emirate traditions as a government public broadcasting institution. Over the past two years it is has transformed itself into a leading global Arabic content provider. It has increased the number of TV channels from two to 10, launched a highly respected English daily newspaper, *The National*, and also set up a number of new media businesses with global presence to take advantage of the digital evolution. One of the specific aims of the organization, whose main stakeholder is the government of Abu Dhabi, is to 'put Abu Dhabi on the global map', bring best-in-class technology and talent to the state and build a local media industry through knowledge and skill transfer to local Emiratis. It is in a unique position since most Western media firms are struggling with spiralling costs potentially threatening their survival. ADMC, on the other hand, is willing to pioneer new enterprises.

Whilst many multinationals have restructured around siloed, core cost centres for closer control, the emerging market organizations are looking to build dynamic, flexible organizations which take advantage of new technology or cross-business synergies. But some of the larger organizations in the emerging markets of Brazil, the Middle East, Indonesia and China which were public institutions in the past still need change as they try to shrug off the baggage of bureaucracy. Their advantage is that they now have been given the licence to make these changes as they move into private sector operations and have the mindset and commitment to do so. Of note in the past 12 months, there has been a shift in focus of some Chinese firms away from Western investment to looking at opportunities in the East, in their homeland of China or other countries such as Vietnam.

New world leadership

Creating new structures requires leadership to drive the changes forward. As the world moves out of recession there is a need to refresh and renew the most senior managers. After all, many of them oversaw the policies and practices that led to the overgearing, credit-fuelled expansions that led us into the crisis in the first place.

The new world leader will need better balance. A recent White Paper by Mercer Delta ELC with Economist Intelligence Unit, entitled 'The global

FIGURE 9.2 A new management framework: second building block

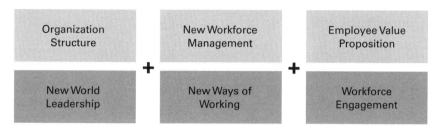

leadership imperative: capturing competitive advantage'[2], proposes the four-dimension model of required capabilities shown in Figure 9.3.

The new leaders will need to use their heads to overcome complexity by helping to articulate clear vision, assess strategy and take a broader picture through a global mindset. In terms of heart, they will need to lead others by example and with passion; they also need to speak from the heart and have the ability to recognize diversity and thereby speak across the whole organization. Guts represent courage, thereby requiring new leaders to be able to lead change by building capability, removing obstacles but with both tenacity and integrity. Finally, the hands are needed to deliver results and ensure effective completion and evaluation.

Another facet of the new leader is the requirement to be emotionally intelligent. The predominant leadership model from the 1950s to the millennium was one of a command and control mindset: telling employees what to do. It was founded on a hierarchical business structure with formal authority and top-down decisions. This directive style was based on individuals earning their supervisory power from having delivered a previous track record of results and a focus on the numbers – in conclusion, a style best summed up as micro-management. These individuals still exist today, of course, and the retrenchment of the past year or so, unfortunately, has brought many of these traits back to the fore.

Going forward in a world with greater global interactions which are more complex, faster moving and high tech, the new leader will need to hold multiple perspectives, provide more coaching and allow employees more space, more delegation and more empowerment. Part of this will be a natural outcome of dealing with a more diverse workforce with high expectations as outlined earlier. New leaders will need to articulate a compelling, shared vision to ensure active engagement by employees and hence will need to be very self-aware of their own behaviour and its impact on others. Consequently, these new leaders will need to display greater emotional, social, interpersonal and multicultural skills to communicate with an ever-widening group of stakeholders. They must be at ease to

FIGURE 9.3 The new world leader

Leaders need to be able to draw from the head, heart, guts and hands

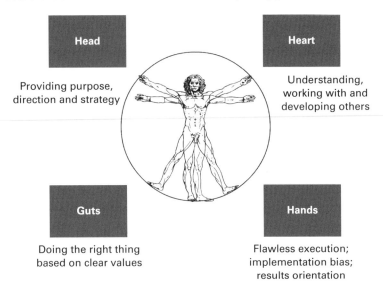

Head	Heart
Providing purpose, direction and strategy	Understanding, working with and developing others

Guts	Hands
Doing the right thing based on clear values	Flawless execution; implementation bias; results orientation

© Mercer 2010[2]

interact across all levels of the organization and not use seniority or rank to engage the new workforce.[3]

Lateral versus vertical leadership

Within this context the old style of vertical leadership based on reporting hierarchy, with set, controlled processes will give way to a new form of lateral leadership which will see the new leader working through internal and external networks in order to seek out and exploit new opportunities, to identify creativity and innovation, to learn and to build improvement.

Lateral leadership requires three new mindsets. The first is a whole-system, holistic mindset. This requires a switch from an internal to an external, outward focus, primarily to build a customer-centred environment where strategies can be translated into clear priorities and action. It also needs a willingness to learn from experiences to integrate the diverse perspectives and ideas to give a new point of view. This is very much the mindset of our global nomad.

The second shift is to a relationship and partnering mindset. As organizations have retrenched, there has been a tendency for senior management to become more insular, to protect their departments and their current power centres. As the world breaks out of recession, organizations will need to create a new working environment based on internal and external partnerships and working relationships built on trust in order to get shared commitment.

Which leads to the third shift, one towards a more flexible, open mindset. As business becomes more unpredictable with more trade being undertaken in new markets, the new leader will need to be able to deal with more ambiguity and paradox. This will require balancing competing demands and skilfully handling points of disagreement towards win–win outcomes. Dealing with the East takes time as this is how they get to know you, so patience, tolerance and tenacity are also required behavioural competencies.[4]

Lateral leadership implies breaking down the organizational silo mentality. This will be hard for many larger international companies which spent years establishing these divisions. Not only is it possible, it is also imperative if organizations are going to meet the customized demands of our new world and the next generation workforce entering the workplace.

An illustration of the power of lateral leadership occurred at Nike a few years back. In the past, as a customer entering one of their stores you might have been looking to buy a pair of football boots for your son or daughter and would have been directed to the back of the store where footwear was on display. But then you also wanted the latest Brazilian kit, which was over on the far side of the store, in the apparel section. And of course you needed the ball – which was somewhere else, under equipment.

Many customers might not have persevered. So when a middle-level manager suggested there might be another way to group the products by each sport, such as soccer, running, golf, etc, this initially was viewed as challenging to the powerful silo barons. Yet the formula worked so well that sales accelerated tenfold.

Hence the future leader competencies therefore will shift from the Western models towards new emerging Eastern models which will be more fluid, more customized to variation in culture. To date multinationals have been dogmatic in imposing their view of 'one culture', typically based around a Western management model of set values, defined core competencies and a given leadership framework.

I now see organizations wanting to review and revise these processes. A new model is emerging with the characteristics shown in Figure 9.4.

This model pulls together the points raised in this chapter and reflects the necessary shift in balance to personal, people-centred skills of the new leader yet still maintaining a business-driven action focus and a new form of decision making. These competencies are the foundation for selecting the experienced global nomad business leader and will provide the basis for identifying the new breed of high-potentials whom multinational firms must nurture for the future.

FIGURE 9.4 New leader model

- Action focused
- Takes calculated risks
- Multiculturally aware
- Skilled negotiator
- Trusted adviser
- Results through others
- People-centred

SOURCE: 'Leading the change', Jim Matthewman[5]

References

1 Forbes (2010) 'The world's leading companies – Headquarters Inc.', May, pp 96–7, **www.forbes.com**
2 Mercer Delta ELC with Economist Intelligence Unit (2006) 'The global leadership imperative: capturing competitive advantage'
3 Dr Brendan McCann (2010) 'Executive effectiveness: choosing wisely at defining moments'
4 'Leadership in Transition', Jim Matthewman, paper presented at HR Forum, May 2005
5 'Leading the Change', Jim Matthewman, paper presented at Mercer's Asia Pacific Conference, 3 November 2009

New workforce management

10

N ow is the time to realign the organization's people strategy to the fast-changing business needs and, in many cases, a changing business model. The economic crisis has given firms the opportunity to tackle inconsistencies and address misaligned structural, cultural and work practices which have been built up over decades.

In the past 20 years, many of the core people management processes have either been built in isolation or have failed to keep pace with business changes. With a new business focus on the emerging markets, there will be a major pressure to make these critical people processes more flexible and adaptable, thereby able to fit local or regional markets. HR must also be far more agile in its delivery, and its decision process needs to match the pace of the business.

However, whilst many larger firms have taken the opportunity to rein in some of the abuses of the past, to shake out weakness and specifically reduce the cost of people programmes, this is likely to cause rising tension between the firm, the employees and line managers. One of the major fault

FIGURE 10.1 A new management framework: third building block

lines where these tensions will surface will be in the administration of mobility and expatriate policies.

So how should organizations align their people processes to these new business priorities? Over recent years Mercer has developed a strategic perspective which combines business strategy, key dimensions of workforce management and resulting HR programmes as illustrated in Figure 10.2.

Post-recession, organizations are looking for more simplicity, as confirmed by independent research firm Kennedy Consulting Research & Advisory.[1] Mercer has now interpreted this into four main strategy areas, as shown in Figure 10.3.

However, in the emerging markets, the level of HR strategy and practice remains a little bit behind the game, hence most of the transformation projects are CEO or business leader driven, with consultants as often local personnel or HR departments. They have neither the skill nor the capacity to pick up the pace today; but they are learning fast.

The reality is that Western HR jargon typified by 'human capital strategy' has little resonance in these new world markets. Even the biggest European market, Germany, in 2007 voted 'human capital' the worst invented jargon of the year.[2] The emerging markets are full of over-engineered Western management philosophies which in many local firms have failed because they were not tailored or amended to fit local work culture. These include 'forced ranking', the 'extended balanced scorecard' and 'key performance indicators (KPIs)', extended down to every employee. This is the fault of both consulting firms and their clients, who have pursued implementation of 'best practices' as a goal when the real need is 'best fit'.

I have already discussed leadership development, and recognition and reward will be covered in our next chapter. So let us deal with the links between role clarification, performance management and talent management and what this will mean for the increasingly mobile workforce.

As companies both domestic and international sort out their strategies in the new markets, there is a pressing need to match changing organizational design with clear accountability through role definition and execution (note: this is not responsibility and job descriptions).

Role clarification and setting out new performance expectations

What I see is that strategy and top level organization design typically focus on tier 1 (senior executive management team, ie divisional directors reporting to tier 0, the CEO/GM in region). They rarely cover tiers 2 to 4, senior managers (department heads and their direct reports, who might be section managers or the most senior professionals). It is astonishing how many firms in all markets have yet to define the top 100 jobs. But if these folk are not clear on their responsibilities and, more importantly, their accountabilities, one can ask what focus there is for the organization.

FIGURE 10.2 Business strategy, workforce management and HR programmes

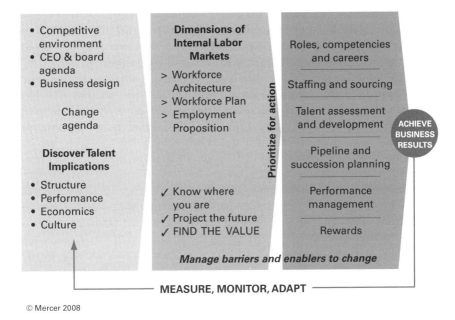

© Mercer 2008

FIGURE 10.3 Four key components of effective people strategies

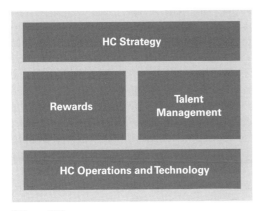

© Mercer 2010

There is a constant demand to build job descriptions for this group and then to extend the process to their reports. This is very old school, as my Generation Y children would say. Asking people to describe and document their current jobs, responsibilities and associated activities will not move the organization forward.

What is needed is to future-scope roles (not jobs) and not in terms of activity analysis or 'responsibilities' but to shift the agenda to what will be the purpose and accountability of future roles (ie specify what is expected in nine to 18 months' time) and what exactly will be different.

This means the focus of job evaluation changes from asking employees to describe their jobs today to asking managers what they expect these roles to deliver in the future. Employees cannot answer this question.

Roles not jobs: what's the difference? Typically, job descriptions are usually produced for two reasons – *either* because the organization has decided to revamp its existing grading structure and pay system because of increasing external market misalignment or internal manipulation, *or* because of individual recruitment needs whereby a line manager has to create a new job description to justify a new or changed post to attract new talent (most often assumed at a higher grade).

Following classic methodology, once a job description is produced, analysed and evaluated and handed over to an employee, it gets buried in the bottom drawer of the desk. It then reappears when a manager makes a request for an additional task, prompting the response that this is not in the specified scope and hence must justify a re-evaluation or regrading of the role even if it had been written years ago. In this sense job descriptions are comfort blankets or, in reality, obstacles to change.

Role profiles are different. If you tell an employee they have a role to play in an organization, it immediately sends a message of purpose and implies the role is part of a bigger picture, a cog in a multifaceted process with an outcome. It also requires the incumbent to be an actor required to take on behaviours as appropriate to customer or client needs.

Roles also imply you are part of a team – your position is pivotal irrespective of grade or seniority. Most sporting teams – soccer, American football, basketball, hockey or handball – rely on a combination of defined roles and skills to execute a game plan. You can have the best fly-half in the world capable of executing a drop goal in the dying seconds of the game (thank you, Jonny!) but it only happened because nine other guys out of the 15 followed a set play to perfection. So we all have a part to play. What happens in the modern world when someone is sick or on vacation? Telling a customer or client (external or internal) that we cannot process their request because 'It's not my job' or that the person responsible is away cuts little ice. As result we need modern roles to imply team cover and collaboration. To maintain the company's customer excellence promise, staff not only need to know their own roles in detail but also those of others around them. So role profiles need to be extended to a wider remit but with a bit more focus than the traditional 'and other duties or requirements as determined by your supervisor'.

What this provides is agility and adaptability. Employees are clear that there is a foundation framework but it has flexible boundaries based on agreement and trust that the process will not be abused – a clear adult-to-adult understanding. Managers in turn get more wriggle room to make things happen, and the unit delivers. Such a scenario for a 1960s–1970s worker would have drawn major resistance but for our new nomadic Generations X and Y workforce, who have grown up with constant change and challenge, this is seen as an opportunity to shine: yet another experience to bag. If only their line managers could let go and free their passion and energy without the micro-management centred on reporting minutiae to protect the 'plan'.

Role profiling has a second feature which is music to CEOs' ears. By breaking out of the set description of task, we can also talk of role progression. This is development and advancement *within* a given role, not some phoney promotion based on a marginal change in responsibilities or more commonly length of service. The latter assumes that if a person has spent five, 10 or 15 years in the same role they must have acquired added-value experience to justify a promotion (assuming they have built up skills and capability to undertake more complex and demanding work). In truth, there are many employees who have not progressed and have not given the commitment to provide extra value, and hence may have only contributed one or two years' effort 20 times. Yet they have been promoted because of loyalty and tenure. Many firms now openly say they would be happy to replace such a person with one, two or three younger, passionate recruits, knowing they will get five to 10 times the productivity at the same cost or less.

When I first started to review job evaluation 28 years ago I was struck by the inertia created by job descriptions and as I then researched skills and competencies I became convinced by line managers and employees that a simple progression model exists in every role.

Over time I have been lucky to work with over 2,000 different organizations in 30-plus different countries and have analysed or reviewed literally millions of jobs and feel justified in claiming the following is true, readily accepted by senior and line managers as good common sense.

Ask any manager of a sizeable team (eg a customer service manager) the following: if they had to recruit a new customer service representative tomorrow, what would be the four or five key accountabilities, necessary skills and experience and indeed, in their mind, the requisite personal attributes for the job (typically described as a team player, good communicator, proactive, problem solver and so forth)? What they would be describing is the proficient employee meeting the objectives of the role (the basis for a role profile and role evaluation).

But in reality it is extremely rare that anyone is able to step into a new job from day one and be fully proficient. They need to understand the company's processes and procedures, their target customers, 'the way of doing things around here', and specific product or service skills. When asked how long it takes for technical, professional or managerial roles to get up to speed, ie to be fully proficient, nearly every manager says between six and nine months. Hence they have a concept of entry and development in the role. Whilst I have heard some say this can be 12 months, the reality is that few organizations and department managers can wait more than nine months for individuals to be fully effective; if they claim longer, the company clearly needs to re-examine its entry and recruitment criteria.

If I then ask whether in this group of similar employees there are any individuals who could be considered as 'advanced', nearly all line managers will say 'Yes, I have two or three of those.' So the obvious question is: what is the difference between these advanced role holders and the proficient, solid contributors? As line managers try to explain the difference, nearly all will describe an ability to consistently outperform objectives, a capability to accept and complete more complex or less defined work, an ability to coach and mentor new folk and deputize for the departmental manager. And most will say it takes at least two to three years to get to such a level. Which of course begs the question of how people move from proficient to advanced levels within a given role? Note that this is not promotion (ie a true movement from one role to another within a given job family whereby the accountabilities are substantially different, the size of responsibilities significantly greater and the overall role larger). Many will quote an aptitude to undertake more complex work, self-learning and a willingness to go beyond the role accountabilities, to work across other departments and participate in cross-functional project teams looking for innovation or process improvements.

So virtually all managers are walking around with this model inside their head but rarely express it to their employees. But what a fantastic motivator it would be if role incumbents could understand what is expected and what it takes to move to the next level. Furthermore, if this could be consistently described across the organization, we would then have the basis for a fairer, competency-based progression in base pay rather than seniority or years of tenure.

There are three additional benefits to the organization. First, as Figure 10.4 depicts, once a role holder consistently displays the performance, skills and competencies of an advanced role holder, then there is an odds-on chance that they can step up to the demands of a bigger job as many of these attributes will be the baseline for a proficient role holder in the next level. Too often promotions are awarded because they are:

- a defence mechanism in a potential key talent exit;
- a means to reward years of loyalty in a role, even though individuals may have only delivered one year's work for 10 or 15 years;
- reward for high performance even though we have little guarantee that they will deliver at the higher level.

Second, this model highlights the area of added value beyond being simply proficient in a given role. Third, organizations need to take advantage of such tools to future-proof roles and hence set out how a given role will play to the future strategy. Providing clear feedback and guidance will help set out the new added value. It allows managers to articulate the stretch required

FIGURE 10.4 Understanding role progression

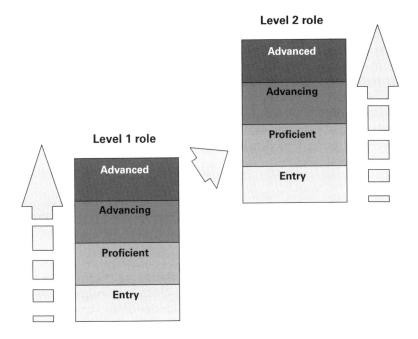

to progress both within a given role and in new roles both vertically and laterally within the firm. This is the foundation to building effective career management in a changing world.

This will have significant value for the new generation workforce and the global nomads in particular. This generation are looking for clarity around performance expectations and how quickly they can outperform. This is a group who want to move fast and receive recognition for their contribution and output. This does not mean promotion or status per se but a clear message of what is expected, with regular honest feedback that they are moving forward in line with peers. These models of progression provide a better basis for such discussions. What is important to the nomads is the transparency of process – a challenge for most organizations in the way they have dealt with employees in the past. After all, this is a generation which has outperformed at each level of education – they are armed with qualifications and desperate to prove their personal and collective contribution.

This is a creating a potential and very real issue for multinationals. As the recovery takes hold in the emerging markets, fuelled by the agile talents of the nomads and their high-energy focus, there is a growing imbalance between the performance of these units and these vibrant, younger professionals in comparison with those based in the mature markets. The latter, in part, are stifled by big company policy and the legacy of set, corporate ways plus the limited opportunities available in their markets. This is not to say they are less talented or committed, but for various reasons they have not been able to participate in the pace and scale of emerging market opportunities.

There is growing pressure that outperforming performance ratings of emerging market personnel will spotlight the relative average performance of similar peers or even seniors in home markets. The real danger is that the corporate beast then tries to apply overall averaging to 'balance' ratings and force fit into 'normal, forced distributions' on the basis of reconciling investments in these emerging regions when the mature markets carried the risk of previous years. This demand is viewed as a hollow argument by today's mobile workforce.

Performance calibration in high-performing companies

The famed General Electric (GE) model of performance management (of yesteryear, to be fair, but still stuck in the minds of many managers) with its focus on forced distribution essentially demands action to recognize and reward the overachievers, with less to those failing to meet objectives and removal of the bottom 10 per cent to be replenished by a new crop of eager talent. The model, as most now realize, is flawed as organizations seek out better, higher-potential talent. The forced distribution means removing a valid group of solid contributors simply to meet the numbers. Second, applying it uniformly across an organization penalizes those departments with low headcount but high impact (eg R&D or innovation units) in favour of larger, bureaucratic support functions. This is clearly not what most organizations intended. Likewise, organizations who actively seek out and select higher-qualified or experienced individuals, whether they be an investment bank or leading academic institution such as Harvard, will by definition aim to be higher performing and so the 'normal curve' is already skewed from the outset.

In the emerging markets, the failure of forced ranking is most evident. The imposition of such a blunt instrument to drive performance in regions where performance management is so weak both in managers' ability to set meaningful, measurable objectives and their subsequent ability to fairly assess individual contribution has led to years of blatant, acknowledged manipulation. In such markets where nationalization targets are also obligatory, it makes removal of underperformers, a fair proportion of whom are local nationals, impossible. The end result is two systems: the documented process demanded by group masters and the actual practice which allows managers to blatantly allocate ratings in rotation to their team to ensure a balance of reward and promotion to those loyal over a two- or three-year period that has nothing to do with actual performance.

Two new practices have merged – 'performance calibration' and 'moving the middle'. The first looks to modify business unit performance rating distribution in line with a business unit's actual contribution rather than force-fit a standard curve. Thus there is still a curve but it is now matched to an agreed distribution allocation for a given contribution to the overall corporate achievement. It means that higher-performing units can have a skewed curve towards higher ratings if the senior executive team agrees this is justified. Likewise, those units which have failed to meet expectations would be expected to have a greater number of people in categories below 'meeting target'. Overall the individual unit curves must aggregate to the company's overall performance rating.

The process returns responsibility to business unit leaders both individually and collectively. It allows more objective assessment across a group of employees and can be backed up by cross-functional validation teams or senior management moderation, especially in review of ratings at the extreme (ie outstanding or exceeding or unacceptable performance). For those organizations which have a high degree of sophistication and have experience in setting performance goals and KPIs, this process provides a means to raise the performance bar and ensure the process retains credibility, as illustrated in Figure 10.5.

It can also allow comparison with industry or regional norms, again bringing a greater sense of fairness to the performance assessment process.

FIGURE 10.5 Implementing business unit calibration

- This scenario represents the expected distribution where a business unit performs outstandingly achieving a KPI score of 5.0
- Under the model 7.0% of employees would be rated below 'solid', the number above 'solid' increases significantly to 38.0% reflecting the exceptional nature of business unit performance at this level
- The positive skew seen is out of line with market norms but reflects the exceptional nature of a KPI 5.0 score

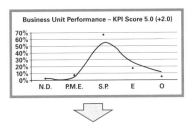

Exceeding	Outstanding
JM, KC, TG, BV, FF, SD, GY, GH, AA, EF, PO, KJ, DD	TY, MV, WW, RE, JD, DF
Solid performer	
OB, OA, MA, MC, SF, TJ, SJ, SO, EP, PP, WE, DF, FG, IU, AS, WD, FG, GH, GR, HN, OP, WF, RT, JH, GD, AL, RT, PD, MG	
Needs development	**Partially meets expectations**
LK	OK, MO, IT

Dealing with underperformance

An alternative is more appropriate where the performance management is largely broken, with a high degree of employee cynicism. In these situations trying to force more differentiation where there is little management or employee buy-in is like pouring oil onto the fire. At best organizations can hope to restart discussion around performance goals and their effective cascade into departmental and individual targets.

In these situations companies need to be explicitly clear about what performance management is and what it is not – and then ensure that all actions demonstrate this.

Directors and departmental managers must openly demonstrate that performance management is a core management activity that involves management time, management passion, management judgement and management accountability. In essence, this requires a mindset shift that performance means 'planning for, working towards and achieving tangible results', ie more than words, it requires a group change in behaviour. Organizations will need to expect all managers to spend dedicated time to plan performance and reflect on achievements at divisional and individual level. Effective performance management should be an explicit performance target for each manager. It primarily moves from a written process to one of guiding conversations where the 'what' that someone achieves is planned for and discussed as well as 'how' they go about achieving it. It also should include elements of wider feedback from team members, subordinates, project/committee members, and ideally customers both internal and external. But, fundamentally, when the performance culture is so poor, the links to reward need to be reappraised. Whilst links with related systems, eg reward or promotion, should be recognized, these links should not be so strong that they overwhelm the whole system. The whole process needs simple-to-use tools to guide people, recognizing that this does not mean a 10-minute conversation once a year but that it takes people management skills to do it well. Once again, it is important for multinationals to recognize that established, mature (sophisticated) performance management systems used elsewhere may fail in the new markets.

However, as our nomad interview input has highlighted, Western multinationals need to rebalance their mature-market-centric thinking to recognize that individuals delivering superior performance in the emerging markets will find it difficult to accept recalibrations (ie down-rated to global normal distributions). This will be risky given the mobility propensity of the nomads and hence attrition, which might destabilize the local office. There is strong evidence that this debate is still struggling to be acknowledged within senior management circles that seem to be in denial of the rise and change in market focus which is already happening.

Moving the middle

The 'move the middle' model can also apply to higher-performance organizations. Here the problem is how to replicate the behaviours of the most successful and turn individual talent into a replicable, scalable model.

Outstanding performers typically display traits which go to the limit of the business model, but in many organizations key players are in this space. They are sufficiently confident that they can stretch the portfolio to encompass a wider customer proposition, create new service offerings, and experiment with licence since they have a track record of delivery. And where better to let these players have space than in the emerging markets where the needs are less defined, customers more open-minded, want to differentiate and to pioneer first-market-mover propositions. Rather than present standard, transactional offerings (which will only get eroded in time by competitive price pressure and 'me-too' lookalikes), these markets offer a chance of a few big bets.

In this scenario, moving the middle has a different context. It focuses on the traits of the highest performers and how they can be bottled up and spread over known solid contributors. As illustrated in Figure 10.6, the hypothesis is that a 5 per cent increase in the middle (ie the 60 per cent of solid contributors) is worth 70 per cent more revenue than a 5 per cent shift of the star performers (the top 20 per cent).[3]

For many major multinational firms the role of star performers is difficult, if not uncomfortable. In the 1990s Western doctrine, these were dangerous individuals, rule breakers, going beyond process and procedures for personal gain, and difficult to replicate in standard business development methodology. Firms were right to reel in these individuals to prevent market abuse when, at extreme levels, the organization lost governance and risk management.

However, in the same action, some have overreacted, and in doing so they also killed off much of the entrepreneurialism, courage and inspirational leadership which many younger potentials need. Some professional firms have retrenched into a safe cocoon based on regulated, transactional day-to-day activity which will struggle to deliver shareholder expectations as such a model erodes profit margins given lack of market differentiation and price competitiveness. In the worst case, the danger is that the organization then loses spirit and hence the passion to excel. Everything is driven by process and ultimately fails to engage both employees and customers.

But star performers are difficult to manage. They are high maintenance yet they have the ability to shape markets, create noise and simultaneously engage externally and internally. Their track record shows that they have magic pixie dust. Setting aside the geniuses who dream up new formulae, products and service solutions, the real issue here is those who deal with the customer interface, ie the business development and sales professionals,

FIGURE 10.6 Moving the middle

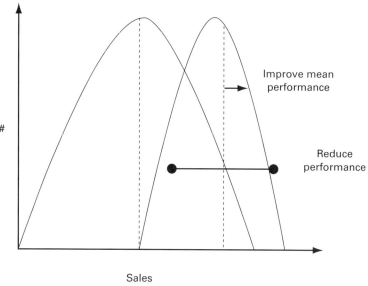

marketers and customer service managers who concoct, identify and then manage relationships and retain customer loyalty. In the next five years, the CEO and HR leaders in the corporate interviews outlined in Part Five have said that these will be the key differentiating professionals for their organizations. It will not be the technologists or the product manufacturers, as these can be easily replicated if not outsourced for cost-delivery optimization. Instead they will need more 'people-to-people' experts who create external and internal networks and continuing, expanding revenue streams. They will be the new world gold. Organizations need to come up with a compelling proposition for these people whilst recognizing the growing mobility of this group.

But not everything that stars do is exceptional. They typically are very focused in time and effort (and hence high performers not because they do twice as much as others in a working day but because they are able to create enough time to do twice as much 'new work' in the same time – they will deliver 150 per cent of what solid, standard employees deliver. This is partly because they are focused – they utilize their time efficiently – but also because they are passionately committed to the work they do (actually beyond their firm) to a higher professional, spiritual level. For those organizations who want to seriously outperform the market, the key is to get this star essence into the bottle and sprinkle it on other willing contributors.

When I presented this concept to the CEO of a European high-tech organization, his reaction was interesting. His analogy was political voting. He said he spent approximately 40 per cent of his time trying to rescue seriously dissatisfied customers because all efforts by his sales or customer support teams were failing. In his political analogy, these 'customer voters' were already lost but his internal forces were desperate to spend inordinate resource to chase lost causes. He spent only 10 per cent of his time on his top customers – partly because he was told they were happy and there was little noise; the claim was that his client management teams were doing a good job anyway – but significantly he was isolated from them.

So that left the 'floating customers' in the middle, who were not sure whether to commit their business, were under significant pressure to switch to more attractive competitor offers, or were unsure where the organization's priorities lay (not really surprising as the organization's client-facing units were spending proportionately more time serving happy clients who probably were less likely to move away, or a considerably inordinate amount of effort on those likely to move away for ever). His conclusion from the analysis was that he should spend more time on the floating voters – ie the middle – as this had the highest growth potential.

The conclusion, therefore, is to capture what the best sales, marketers or customer service people do and transfer it to the solid contributors serving or prospecting the main body of customers. Second, place a significant basis for reward and recognition of the stars to share and mentor their experience to others in the next two years – and just watch the change in behaviour.

Translating this idea to our emerging markets and the global nomads means that the senior market makers within multinationals or the emerging new world internationals (as perhaps we should call them) need to focus on knowledge transfer from seasoned expats to the new breed of aspiring professionals. This has not happened in the past. Part of the reason is that the tax equalization policies of Western multinationals has meant that these market makers have had to channel all their energy into personal wealth creation from variable bonus schemes, so sharing recognition and success has not been their number-one priority.

The experienced 'most valued player' expats who are crucial in establishing credibility in the emerging markets need to become trusted advisers and ambassadors of the firm. This means that they also need goals and objectives to mentor and coach the aspiring nomads to take the business forward. The latter cannot wait to rise to the challenge. Thus traditional scorecard models of existing multinationals need to place much greater emphasis on the people quadrant and this knowledge transfer with a direct impact on performance rating and associated reward. In this new world, the most valued players need to be open, collaborative midfielders rather than solo strikers building their personal portfolios. The good news, however, is that there is a strong affinity between the Baby Boomers and Generation Y since the former resonate with the passion and energy of the new generational workforce, so hopefully, many will be able to let go and empower the new talent.

The real management, or, to be exact, leadership, issue lies with the middle managers (Generation X) who feel undermined and cheated by the forces of economy and fate. They rightly feel that they have fought battle after battle to carve out personal recognition and their careers only to witness a step change bypassing their individual efforts. This is a difficult circle to square.

More focus on developmental improvement

In this fast-moving emerging world, my personal view is that the emphasis of performance management needs to shift from the dominant results-focused KPI doctrine of the past 10 years to a more balanced business format; note that this does not mean a balanced scorecard. This rarely exists and, sometimes, can completely screw up organizations if over-engineered. What is needed is *a better distribution* of goals across the various scorecard segments; one where results remain paramount but as a wider team event rather than individual focus with a stronger developmental, transformational focus.

This would work on two dimensions. First, we will expect professionals to be more agile, flexible and adaptable to market and customer requirements. This means that the new world professional, schooled in best-practice methodology and process, will be asked to apply their knowledge and experience to provide industry-, regional- and customer-specific insights to their clients and customers rather than generalized set process. More and more organizations can outsource the latter since there is no unique competitive advantage in process and systems. The future centres around people, their experience, creativity and interpretation of local market movements – ie insight. Data alone, even trend analysis – findings – are not enough; as one company told me recently: 'We can do the same in-house; what we need is insight and recommendations.' These are worth paying for.

In pragmatic, practical terms, what does this really mean with organizations increasingly adopting a matrix model of management whereby individuals are likely to have more than one immediate supervisor or are likely to be operating on projects some distance from their office base? It suggests that the professional global nomad needs more feedback and more coaching from senior leaders. This also matches the Generation Y profile of individuals used to constant peer reaction and high recognition needs. Performance management, therefore, cannot be a once-a-year discussion or poorly executed by line managers. It needs systems such as multi-rater feedback or 360-degree processes, which are extremely valuable provided they are regular and constructive. As my interview with Pekka Lundmark, CEO of Konecranes (see Part Five) highlights, it will require senior and middle managers spending more time on people management to ensure effective engagement of this group.

Learning and development in the emerging world

The analysis in Chapter 3 highlights that the demands of the emerging markets require more local insight, more customization, more face-to-face experience. Technical ability is largely assumed or expected and is less of a differentiator as professional standards become industry and global norms. Best practices are important but not as important as best-fit implementation. Understanding local ways of doing business and the relationships of multicultural interaction are critical competencies.

Matched, too, with the thirst for knowledge and desire for challenging experiences from Generations X and Y, learning and development move from classroom, formal training to a much more business-orientated on-site focus. Clearly there are more risks involved as individuals are both given more empowerment and a right to 'experiment', but this is within the context of customer or client partnerships with a mix of shared learning. It requires greater delegation and trust from functional leaders as they shift from the micro-management of detail and reporting. Genuine regular feedback, brainstorming and problem solving are the key processes. Post-project reviews or 'lunch and learn sessions' also become important as a way of capturing and sharing knowledge with wider internal teams in customer- or client-facing roles.

This requires creative programmes of real value to participants through face-to-face knowledge transfer. It also needs commitment. Too often organizations will set up the notion for such sessions but then fail to provide the time and space for the seasoned professionals to interact with the younger workforce to make the sessions a reality.

Yesterday's managers must resist personally diving in to fix problems, thereby giving their teams time and space to resolve issues themselves. This will be a major challenge for many existing senior managers who have got where they are through personal delivery rather than collective effort.

Our case study featuring Batelco (see Part Five) illustrates a structured response to learning, taking account of the mix of generations, different learning styles and the growing internationalization of business.

For this to work, the office environment will need to be very open with all professional levels available and approachable. Cross-functional task forces and innovation groups should be actively encouraged as a way of building multi-disciplined knowledge sharing to break down operational silos. This is one of the fundamental differences between emerging market learning and previous Western styles. In the past 10 years, Western firms have placed responsibility for learning on individuals, asking them to build and shape their careers. In contrast in the East, and China most notably, learning is more a collective, collaborative activity at work, in leisure and in society more generally. This in part explains their rapid pace of economic development and recovery.

References

1 Kennedy's HR Consulting Research Series, *HR Consulting Marketplace 2010–2013*
2 'Shifting the Performance Curve', SEC Solutions, Corporate Executive Board 2004
3 German TV quote

Managing today's global talent

11

In 2007, talent management was on the top of every CEO's agenda. With 10 years of unparalleled growth, finding key talent was the number-one priority. The mature markets found a dearth of home-grown, critical operational skills – notably those of engineers, project managers, chemists and marketers. In part these disciplines had lost out to the glamour of City bankers, lawyers and professional services. Business was booming in both home and emerging markets and whilst some areas of operation, notably customer service call centres and IT, could be outsourced to lower-cost countries such as India and the Philippines, local universities simply were not generating enough qualified graduates in core production, design and manufacturing skills. As a result, many had to resort to importing skills from the developing world, new Europe (Hungary, Poland, Romania, Croatia and Turkey) and MENA (Middle East and North Africa: Lebanon, Jordan, Egypt and Algeria). Pre-Lehman talent flows were strongly from developing countries to the money of the mature markets. See Figure 11.1. CEOs were asking the following questions:

Where is our existing talent?

Have we got the right talent for the future?

The impact of demographics – how do we engage 'the engine room'?

Where are the market hotspots?

Where are tomorrow's leaders?

How will we cope with globalization, mobility and diversity?

FIGURE 11.1 Previous expat movement – longitudinal mobility

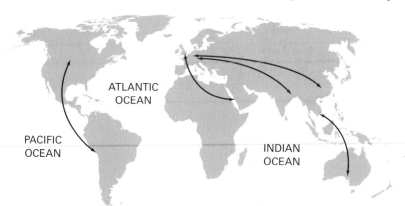

These questions are still relevant today post-recession. It is just there are other priorities at present as organizations try to rebuild a sustainable business model in a world with more volatility. The new issue will be that, as economies move out of recession, the pace of talent acquisition and retention will be much faster than before.

What we are now seeing is latitudinal mobility as individuals move from one assignment to another within the broad band of the tropics. See Figure 11.2.

Over the next few years, the Western multinationals will have new, stronger regional competitors to deal with whose employment proposition may be more attractive to the new generation workforce, ie the global nomads. As a new study from WorldatWork shows, the world's mobile worker population will pass the 1 billion mark in 2010 and will grow by 20 per cent by 2013. This will then be more than one-third of the world's workforce. The most significant gains will be in Asia-Pacific, given the strong recovery. This will not be a time for complacency.

Why is global talent management so important?

Since the 1990s, there has been a growing importance of key talents in driving business success as high-value sectors rely on increasing knowledge and service-based economies. Key talents bring passion, high engagement and excellence in their work and, therefore, are a source of value and competitive advantage. Furthermore, key talents serve to differentiate

FIGURE 11.2 To a new dimension – lateral global nomads

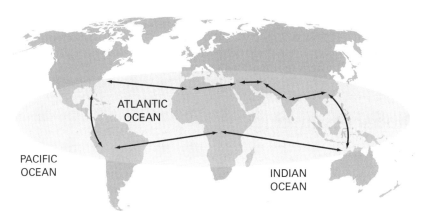

organizations from their competitors, especially in markets where personal relationships drive business trade.

Talent skills have changed from time-served craft skills (where it was commonplace for technicians and engineers to need three to four years' vocational experience to build on educational qualifications) to computer, telecom and customer-facing skills, all of which are transferable. As organizations look to the emerging markets, the key talents in demand are senior sellers and customer relationship managers, innovators – especially in brand and product marketing – technical or production experts, senior operational managers and those capable of being credible country heads (see the case study interview with Dr Nasser Mareth, Group CEO of Qtel International in Part Five).

Companies are now saying that the differentiating skills of key talents are: innovation and thought leadership; superior relationship management and the ability to lead high-performing teams (again see Part Five). These skills are highly transferable between competitors and across industries. As a result employers have to be more sophisticated and successful in attracting key talents. At the same time, regional and global expansion has created more choices for the talents, especially when their home market firms have closed the door on the classes of 2008 and 2009. For many of these graduates, the sensible option encouraged by their Baby Boomer parents was to go out and travel, experience the world and make themselves more compelling to employers via character rather than pure qualifications. For many of Generation Y, this gave them the platform to gain confidence in dealing with different cultures, to identify a sense of purpose through volunteering, and to make independent decisions and experience hard financial choices to survive.

The role of talent management is to identify future leadership talent by spotting those with proven internal leadership talent and those with potential. In doing so, organizations need to target developmental opportunities to the right individuals, which means providing the appropriate exposure to business challenges and experiences and providing opportunities to take risks and try out new ideas. In the current retrenchment, the latter opportunities have sadly been cut out and may take some time to return in the Western multinationals.

Global resourcing

The first need, of course, is to attract the right talent. In an increasingly mobile employment market, this means tapping into the networking world of the global nomad – although for many organizations it is about picking out the young potentials that are already in your firm (interns or graduate intake, the young professionals of two or three years' experience) and facilitating the move. Whilst this might seem obvious, many multinationals make heavy weather of such moves even though the costs are relatively minor. In the main, the majority of the assignees will be either volunteers or operational professionals (ie the nomads) who will only need the offer plus a package to include assistance with the initial transfer, housing and usually transport. However, in practice, the internal processes (HR and finance) seem to transcend into the most complicated bureaucracy, often involving third-party 'relocation specialists' whose agendas seem to be quite at odds with the business need and original intentions. Thus, what seemed a simple move can take six to nine months to organize and then up to four to six months to bed in once the assignee is in place. Most mobility expat policies, if they exist, were written in the 1990s to address movement of senior executive assignments and are totally inappropriate for the business needs and individual expectations of the employee. There are very few assignees that do no have a horror story to relate.

If companies are looking for external new seasoned talent to recruit (typically to manage or input technical specialism into a current project), then a wider scan is necessary. Contrary to many firms' understanding, there is a wealth of data across the world but it is scattered and fragmented. The trick is find the pockets of skilled professionals in one or more countries and then work out the employment proposition to move them to where the work needs to be carried out. Very often the decision will centre around how the company will prepare and execute the transition, taking account of the person's individual needs and addressing family considerations. Again this is often an area in which multinationals struggle and outsource to a third party. Sometimes this can create greater problems as the emotional link to the employer is broken. In fact, it is less about the money but more about the communication, continued management interest and ongoing relationship. This is particularly true of 'hardship countries' where individuals are being asked to perform in extreme or life-threatening situations, or where conditions or cultures are significantly different. Whilst money will solve many of the issues, the pastoral care and level of detail spent in respect of extended family will be critical.

Spotting and attracting talent is also about timing. In many of the global sourcing projects that Mercer has undertaken to identify pools of critical talent around the world, the defining factor is often tapping into the talent pool at a given moment in individual careers. For one European multinational we had identified three key sources for future engineers. Close to home, Italian engineers were a good bet, partly because some organizations in complementary yet different industries were in a serious state of implosion. But for bringing in graduate talent, the recommendation was to target specific universities and screen young graduates in *ingegneria gestionale* (engineering management) for internships prior to graduation. However, it would be important to make it clear at hiring, and even before, by campaigning at selected universities that the best system engineers would be offered the opportunity to have international assignments two years after hiring as a normal part of their personal and career development path. At that point the organization should look beyond the two years for a short-term international assignment to improve both technical and foreign language proficiency. For more experienced engineers the recommendation was to focus on PhDs from universities from Milano and Torino with offers of international assignments and, in doing so, build up the image of the company as an international, not a national, brand. The point here was to concentrate on building up internship offers in the final year of students' university studies up to two years before final qualification as a '*diligentsia*', since after this they become almost impossible to move within Italy, let alone to another country.

In Asia, and China in particular, career moves for male individuals who are 30 or older are nearly always dominated by the wives. In the United States it can be harder to move an individual from one southern city to another than place them abroad.

Develop a Generation Y programme

To get your full share of the new talent, if not more, it is important to tune into Generation Y's vibe by creating a compelling image which has a global mindset at its heart. For the organization above, the recommendation was to create a fast-track programme whereby each of the 12 locations in the home market would hire five multinational employees who could create a multinational community of 60 people, who could act as ambassadors to targeted universities. This community of young talents across the world was to be linked via a dedicated website, virtual events and international working assignments to become future ambassadors of the programme. Most important for this Generation Y group was that they would be offered global or regional contracts with a specific role in the final year at a targeted site. All of this was backed up by a standard on-boarding programme with clear career paths mapped out, six-monthly reviews and supported by a buddy programme initiated with second- or third-year experienced graduates plus three or more other international young talents, so creating an immediate network of at least five people.

On a similar basis the Indian multinational Tata Group runs a progressive 'Ignite' programme. Currently employing some 350,000 employees worldwide, it aims to recruit some 10 per cent of its workplace each year from tier 1 and tier 2 global universities. The campaign is a multicultural programme focused on action-centred learning and technical skills. Uniquely the programme actively involves family stakeholders and guarantees a foreign placement. Its innovative format not only provides business and English language modules, it builds on the global mindset by using art and music as key multicultural bonding tools.

Global nomads are an interesting breed to manage – they want flexibility especially around work–life balance (a real adult relationship of give and take) but they need a high degree of structure to ensure their efforts are channelled and recognized.

They need clear instructions and deadlines but they resent micromanagement. This means that the nomads are quite prepared to stay on to hit the deadline, at the cost of last-minute adjustments to personal arrangements (this is all part of the spontaneity which their social network connectivity endorses) but it is on tacit agreement that a strict office hours/environment culture is relaxed. 'Life–work balance' is more important to this group. For some Western country management cultures this is challenging.

To get the best of this breed, organizations need to give them space to be creative, organize their personal space, listen to music whilst they work (this is how they have always studied) and mix up the teams regularly. As a boss, the key is that you first need to be a mentor and give them the trust and belief to reach exceptional results. One of our best Generation Y talents said to me, 'I'm struggling with multiple requests and projects. I know I can cope but can you give some guidance on what and how I should prioritize?'

As a highly social breed they need to let off steam; they need a pulsating work environment which is professional but at the same time sufficiently laid back and has fun. It is a pity that some multinationals, in the light of the recession, decide that 'fun' is no longer a corporate value. This might need to be revisited.

Learning and development also typically take a hit in any recession. The new nomads, with their insatiable appetite for experiences, plus their multitasking abilities, need first-class learning to engage them. Their pace of change means that their span of attention is very short – learning needs to be very focused, multi-media, hands-on (again, see our case study on Batelco in Part Five), and then let them loose to apply it.

Peer focus groups are key. Let management set a series of issues which need to be addressed and fixed. Then tell them what is the most urgent, set parameters they can work within and let them brainstorm. The nomads will be happy to take ownership and their enthusiasm will be contagious throughout the office.

Young nomads are a different breed; they want feedback but take criticism hard – much harder than managers realize: they can be very tough on themselves. But in most cases there is a tenacity which allows them to make the life choices to be a nomad – hence they bounce back quickly for the next challenge. Just do not let them down too often.

New ways of working

Our previous chapters have clearly set out the argument for a new way of doing business, a new set of workforce values and a new working environment. Combined, these reflect a mindset change, one which is focused on new opportunities and on building growth from the emerging markets as a prime business strategy rather than as an afterthought.

Larger organizations are keen to promote the idea that theirs is a 'great place to work'. Modern work has encroached into people's daily life because in our new 24/7 lifestyles we as consumers expect services on tap, when we require them. We expect ATMs to be fully operational; we expect internet services to be available at any time; we are increasingly expecting 'core' shops – petrol stations, fast-food restaurants and convenience stores – to be open throughout day and night. Business operations can no longer work to local five-day weeks. Time zones intervene; some line managers do not stop to think about the implications of arranging a 'town hall' (an all-employee meeting) for global colleagues or an international client conference call at 8 am on a Friday. They remain oblivious to the fact that in the Islamic world (which now makes up 25 per cent of the world's population) this is not only the weekend but it is also the time for weekly prayers. If multinationals are

FIGURE 11.3 A new management framework: fourth building block

to be successful in the emerging markets, they will need to change their middle-manager mindset fast. Whilst many have changed their image, their brand and their mission, vision and values, they have not embedded the new thinking into their seasoned line managers. This is a where a culture shift is required.

I love those maps which show New York, London, Paris or Berlin as the centre of the world with far-flung countries and other cities mere pin pricks on the global map. It is time to see something with Beijing, Shanghai, Mumbai, Abu Dhabi, São Paulo as the centres of our new modern daily universe.

So the first big change must be the global mindset, with a major programme in multinationals to educate and change behaviour in their senior and middle managers. I recommend all readers to view a video posted on YouTube called 'ThisisChange – Human Capital Edition 2009'.[1] Every day I find managers stunned by these statistics. It is not surprising given most are operating in a closed bubble when their organizations have failed to give them space to see what is happening around them.

The message from this video is all about the pace of change. With retrenchment, some organizations have swung back into 'control mode' but have seemingly overreacted when it comes to consumer and customer markets. They are advocating a message of ultra caution and risk aversion, which, given recent history and shareholder nervousness, is understandable but means the organizational mindset has completely flipped to internal control. Even today for many companies this is probably six, 12 or even 18 months away from full implementation, adjusting to recovery and opportunities of growth. But if Western multinationals want to regain their share of the booming recovery east of Cairo, they need to start identifying key players and change agents who can be the foci of a new message. At present I see many organizations rebalancing their workforces in terms of structure and numbers but few are paying sufficient attention to the manager and employee mindset. This will be critical, as many of these people are the survivors. These employees were told to move from a growth, rose-tinted world and to buckle down. Now they are about to be asked to flip again into even faster, high-growth activity. This is a huge ask to make of a damaged, hurt employee population.

Once again the good news is that on the doorstep is a vibrant new generation waiting to be engaged – but they too come with a chastening mistrust of Big Business and society at large. Many will have felt the pain of the recession and unemployment of six to 18 months – this was not what they as the 'golden generation' were promised. The big message here is that the employment proposition or psychological contract between employer and employee is weaker than ever. Organizations should not take anybody for granted in the post-Lehman world – because whatever the major organizations think and whatever their most senior managers who survived believe, the reality is that the deepest recession for the past 75 years has left a massive dent. Loyalty to the firm cannot be guaranteed.

Corporate targets in the new world

I have already discussed corporate missions and visions in the new world, which are key to setting the new agenda. Most of my work in this area consists of dealing with boards and senior managers who are Baby Boomers or Generation X, and who are blinkered to the reality. They struggle with the pace of how economic and political events are unfolding; given this and their experience of the past 24 months, they are nervous about giving any commitment to business plans or targets. This is potentially creating widespread abdication of accountability or ownership of goals.

For 2011 and the next four years, these targets are being greeted with a degree of disbelief locally in terms of stretch targets as they are being set at the upper limit with the assumption that cost savings locally will mean an equal position in the market. But this fails to realize that everybody else is pouring resource into these emerging markets to gain market share, hence creating a highly competitive market. The high returns of the new markets are no longer assured.

As my interviews with both the nomads and the corporates show, there is a growing disconnect between head office and reality on two grounds. First is the corporate faith that their top customers and clients in the mature markets will deliver 80 per cent of revenue and associated contribution. These customers and clients are themselves looking for cost savings and hence are squeezing the margin wallet. Second is the belief that the emerging markets will continue to contribute 33 to 40 per cent of the overall revenue and even higher contribution and profit in the future. These assumptions should be reappraised.

The message is clear. There is more ambiguity in the equation – the idea of New York, London, Frankfurt or Tokyo simply setting out targets or pricing on an assumption that HQ has devised a global plan without sufficient input from the emerging markets will not work and will fail to make sense. Increasingly these organizations need to take more insight and cognizance of regional market management in setting strategy and annual plans. Market volatility suggests that a half-year or even quarterly review and correction would be prudent mainly because decision cycles have now become significantly longer in the New Normal. Whilst this is very difficult for the mature markets, it is not unusual in the emerging markets. Here the trends over the last few years have actually been not dissimiliar.

So my main message is: recognize the role and contribution of the emerging markets. Yet some senior managers in the mature markets see this as a threat or failure through comparative underperformance of their own units that is likely to impact their personal performance, recognition and reward. Hence why they fight so hard – but the world has changed; the rules are different now.

As we noted in Chapter 6, some multinationals and emerging regional firms are now amending their corporate mission, vision and values statements to reflect new world thinking.

What is interesting here is that the Western 'apple-pie' statements of previous frameworks covering teamwork and integrity are being replaced by more proactive, emotionally inspiring values reflecting new ways of working to raise the game and widen horizons to the new markets. Some examples are:

Curiosity: characterizes an attitude of awareness and looking ahead, of being attuned to others, refusing to accept preconceived ideas and models, and imagination.

Agility: synonymous with vitality, energy, speed, flexibility and adaptability.

Creativity: we thrive on innovation and originality, encouraging risk taking and divergent voices.

Customer focus: we value our customers, putting their needs and interests at the centre of everything we do.

Agility: we move quickly, embracing change and seizing new opportunities.

What is clear is that:

Professionals in the West will soon have to realize that they are no longer the authors of all ideas and best practice. [These] will increasingly come from China and India. This will be a shock for many and will require new attitudes of openness and acceptance.

This means that a deal needs to be worked out with the new mobile workforce, which some of the old timers might find more difficult. This is primarily around flexibility. Nomads, Generation X and Generation Y are looking for more variation and more accommodation to meet their lifestyle needs. This is reflected in terms of working hours, office dress and access to social and professional websites. But as organizations look to do more business in the emerging markets, they need to do more to prepare individuals with 'acceptable life' in a new country. This is more than the formal induction; it needs to have a strong emphasis on multicultural understanding with real-life inputs and experiences, not just broad principles. As business becomes more globally connected, organizations may need to reconsider office environments. Open plan has been good to make all levels approachable but with more reliance on teleconferencing and future video conferencing, most offices just do not have enough quiet places to make these effective.

As we see from the corporate interviews in Part Five, there will be increasing consolidation and standardization of technology and intellectual capital (IC) – originally a first-mover advantage – towards employees as the key differentiator. Too many firms still think their concepts, designs and products are protected IC but in reality most are combinations of the ever-widening global, virtual, intellectual and professional mix circulating at an ever-increasing pace in countries with looser controls.

In the past, multinationals have relied on trademarks, patents and intellectual protocols. In today's world these are being severely tested (for example, through the rise of 'generic drugs' in India or auto product and manufacturing designs in China). In truth the real knowledge is the minds and networks of their senior professionals, high potentials and market-facing relationship managers.

Forward-looking CEOs recognize this. Hence why they place less value on technology or products (as these will be quickly eroded or replicated as unique differentiators), reverting instead to the people dimension. In fact, most of those interviewed agree that employees will remain the key differentiator in 10 years' time. Hence why they want to do something about it now, especially as we know the expected tenure of the new generation is likely to be a maximum of four to six years.

The global nomad deal

12

The global nomads are looking for a new deal, one which matches pay expectations in terms of recognition and reward but also one which has career advancement and opportunities explicitly identified. Pay remains important; in particular, the tax-free element and the housing and travel allowances are key components, but these will vary from location to location.

Organizations need to apply more flexibility to this group if they are going to capture and retain their nomads. These people are likely to be well informed about comparative packages both internally and externally and will quickly assess their overall total reward offer. We also know they are more spontaneous than previous generations, which will require organizations to be more proactive.

As one of my Mercer colleagues states, 'This has been talked about for a long time but multinationals will need to create new reward and career propositions to enable older employees to downshift – to continue working but with reduced responsibility and pay as the last of the Baby Boomers will not be given the option of early retirement but will still have plenty to offer. The trick is how to do this with dignity.'

FIGURE 12.1 A new management framework: fifth building block

Another subject-matter specialist states: 'There are growing concerns about career progression amongst Generation X because the Baby Boomers can no longer retire early to make way for the next generations. This will make Generation X increasingly restless – there is talk of a tsunami of CVs about to hit the market when the signs of recovery are confirmed.'

My nomad research reinforces this viewpoint that this group will be the first to take the risk to leave for jobs offering more experiences and progression, thereby sending global shock waves around the world.

Rewarding the global nomads

In today's economic environment, cost containment is the main focus of attention for the multinationals. This means reviewing the business assumptions of what expat resources are needed, in which locations, and the packages required to make it happen. As our case study of Barclays plc (see Part Five) points out, Barclays 'will still seek out the same level of commitment but there will no longer be a single set of characteristics or a one-size employment proposition. Instead [Barclays] expects a number of different types of workers – some whom the bank will want to keep for 15 years and some specialists for up to five years.'

However, organizations do recognize that there is continued globalization of particular functions, notably in supply chain management, marketing, project management and shared service centres. This requires planning, sourcing and management of these talent segments from a wider, international perspective. The rise of the emerging markets also means that protecting key talents and mission-critical roles is high on the agenda, so the tactical deployment of talent from stagnant markets to more active markets needs pragmatic and speedy decision processes.

However, this short-term focus is in danger of ignoring the growing and more imminent talent flight (now or stored up once conditions improve) which is occurring due to redundancies, salary freezes and bonus curbs. Organizations need to put in place retention plans and address the expat engagement issues detailed later in this chapter. This means that the radar should be focused on potential key skill shortages (eg engineers, marketers, business development professionals and project managers), which might not be the highest priority at the moment but will certainly reappear in the post-recovery phase. As our corporate interviews indicate, there will be a global talent battlefield in the next five years, so firms will need to provide a 'career proposition' now to protect these key skills.

Organizations need to implement an effective mobility programme. Many multinationals will say that they have an 'expat' or 'international assignment' policy and then in the same breath will admit that the programme is largely moribund given that they are now managing by exception in the light of the business pressures of recent years. Surprisingly,

25 per cent of the 243 major multinationals in Mercer's 2009 Expatriate Benefits Survey[1] said they had no policy, even though 49 per cent of these organizations had operations in more than 30 different countries. Some of these policies were drawn up in the 1980s or 1990s and are now seriously out of date. Today, there is a need to build pragmatic, engaging and repeatable international talent processes. Part of the issue stems from poor HR/finance systems to efficiently process and interpret the large amount of data for a widely dispersed population.

The other issue is having senior managers committed to maximize the firm's talent and sufficiently skilled to provide the right on-the-job experiences for the high-potential talents and international assignees. In most companies the lack of a sufficient career infrastructure makes it very difficult to make well-informed decisions across organizational and international boundaries.

Global talent management is about influencing the movement and retention of targeted individuals or groups that you need to deploy or develop internationally for current and/or future business success. This means identifying, deploying and retaining *key* talents across the global operations: creatively looking for new sources of talent and selectively using international movement to build and grow the talent and leadership of tomorrow.

There are significant challenges in managing key international talent through effective assignment life cycles given that once an employee is away they are 'out of mind'. More important is that most firms are still grappling with the question of whether there will be a suitable position in the home country – especially in the newly restructured organization since the higher the level of the employee, the harder it will be to find such a job. This means that career paths must be clarified or redefined. One area often overlooked is one of skills mismatch as the skills and know-how developed during the assignment are not necessarily the ones required for the return job in the home country. This of course is a headquarters view. But as we now know from the global nomad interviews, this is wrong thinking since the return to home country in many cases is not the next destination.

A further complication is a job-level mismatch: the international assignee is often promoted to a higher level than their home country peers or progresses faster, which will lead to difficulties on return. And we know that the nomad expectations – rightly or wrongly – are centred on career advancement, which may remain unrealistic in the new flatter organization hierarchies.

The firm needs a dedicated unit to bring all this together. Often in the past the ownership was placed as a subset of a group compensation and benefits team, yet Figure 12.2 shows that this only covers the cost, terms and conditions of the transfer. With the shift in business focus, the question of international assignment, local-contract expats, global nomads and international resourcing has moved to a more strategic level. HR talent management and resourcing departments are now involved in determining

FIGURE 12.2 Integrating the global mobility components

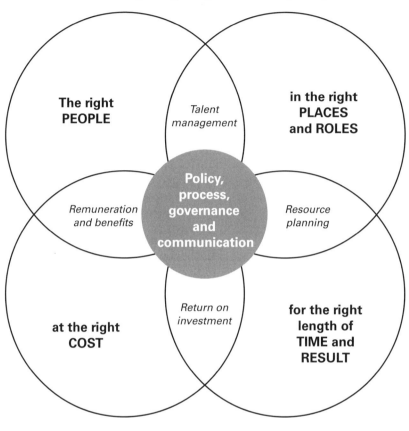

© Mercer 2009

who should be considered. This group should be accountable for the selection process, using talent segmentation and identification techniques, producing candidate profiles and matching the business selection criteria.

Likewise, business leaders have taken the CEO's lead to show a keener interest in international assignments. Their role demands a sharper identification of business need against location, a clear responsibility to differentiate between standard and critical roles and more precision to define the key skill requirements.

This leaves the central unit with the role of governance and policy administration to review the assignment purpose, type and length of assignment, the assignment life cycle management and, most importantly, transition management.

Start-up operations are particularly vulnerable where there is a danger that a significant proportion of staff may be at risk at the same time, either in terms of mass movement to a competitor or via scattered dispersement as these nomadic individuals pursue their aspirations. Occasional staff movements, particularly if these are for vocational or professional development (eg to pursue an MBA), should be positively acknowledged so that individuals leave on a high. This not only will have a major impact on the remaining nomads but will help reinforce the company's employment brand, internally and externally.

Irrespective of base pay and the tax questions which arise, the major concern for expats and the global nomads is associated benefits. The traditional expat model is based on home country social security, inclusive of relevant tax or legal restrictions, notably around occupational pensions and the risk benefits of death, disability or serious injury. Medical plans, however, are usually host-location based.

All of which works well where there is a clear expectation of the individual returning to the home country within five years, as this maintains a given standard and avoids fragmentation of benefits. But now this traditional model is under strain.

As we now see, expatriates and global nomads are being drawn from an increasing range of countries and with little expectation that they will return to their original country of hire. And given that many of these employees are now coming from emerging countries to then work in other emerging markets, they may have inadequate benefits programmes in their home countries or no reciprocal agreements. This is taken further in the case of the growing number of global nomads for whom neither home nor host provisions are appropriate. This has prompted increased levels of localization – ie staff offered local contracts rather than international terms – but this, of course, will carry more risk of attrition. Some firms have reacted by looking to introduce more international plans and more flexibility, even on case-by-case terms.

One of the key terms of high interest for global nomads is medical benefits, but given that the emerging market's host-country facilities are often poor with a lack of social security cover and, in many cases, involve dependants left in a home country, companies have had to respond by offering private international medical cover. But this is costly, so more and more are asking employees to contribute towards the cost of family members through co-insurance.

On balance, therefore, benefit plans are no longer 'one size fits all'. They are becoming more flexible – a hybrid approach – with both regional variations and different options for different expatriate employee groups. However, this is more demanding since it requires a clearly defined policy which allows the flexibility but which carefully documents any exceptions.

What I hear from companies and our interviewees is that multinationals tend to get the larger elements right but fail on many of the smaller details, creating significant levels of frustration – often needlessly. For example, the use of subcontracted relocation companies is usually presented as a benefit to the nomad yet in practice these firms often confuse their role to the nomad with one of cost reduction to the employer.

Many of the issues could be easily avoided by better communication. Besides clear information about the assignment, terms and conditions and tax advice, organizations could do a lot more to provide background data in respect of the target country, its customs and culture, differences in cost and quality of living, and personal calculations of cost projections – especially when inflation rates are becoming more volatile. Once the relocation is under way, more is required in respect of cross-cultural training, spousal support, housing and school search, personal banking, plus visas and permits.

But some of the nomads, too, need to be more realistic and sensitive to their host countries. A few, it seems, assume that their expat package should cover all the expenses abroad, so their base salary can be used for savings. For others, the choice of home or car needs to be more suitable to the local population – driving around in a Hummer or designing lavish gardens or swimming pools might not be the most appropriate local option.

In conclusion, international firms will need to address the continuing failure to communicate policy or overall package components to reduce the noise or discontent amongst the new global nomad population. They also need to ensure the right leadership talent is in place in critical markets to ensure the organization not only survives but can take advantage of emerging business opportunities. For some this will require significant leadership change or management renewal in the key markets.

The message, therefore, is that future mobility management should be a process of repair, process improvement and programme optimization.

Engaging the nomads

The key to motivating the new generation and the global nomads will lie in active engagement. This means providing the necessary challenge to keep this group proactively focused, both physically and mentally.

FIGURE 12.3 A new management framework: sixth building block

Engagement is much more than employee satisfaction. It requires emotion and energy, since this drives 'discretionary' behaviour. It means individuals are prepared to devote extra time, an increased desire to pursue intellectual and professional challenge and, most importantly, high energy. All of which leads to a greater passion for work.

Highly engaged employees bring:

- willingness to go the extra mile for customers;
- creative energy in their work;
- motivation to perform to the highest standard;
- a sense of mutual purpose and excitement;
- pride in the organization.

The new breed of global nomads display all these characteristics. They are looking to push boundaries and secure new market opportunities; the type of work will typically require experimentation, new knowledge and customization, working in cross-functional teams of mixed disciplines and mixed experience but equal respect. Increasingly their work will be project based, working across borders or functional boundaries and with partners from other organizations. Both the nomads and their employers will need to recognize that this deal will be different from other employee groups in their parent organization.

Their buzz comes from the high level of interaction between customer and client teams and internal groups looking for win–win solutions which take product or service propositions to the next level.

Regular, multi-rater feedback (ie from bosses, peers, mentors and customers or consumers) is critical as the group is constantly trying to measure success and progress to a next level on a professional plane. This should not be an annual event but may be fortnightly, monthly or quarterly. In fact, the more informal this feedback, the better. Ideally it should have a clear coaching emphasis. But this has significant implications from current management as this will require more face-to-face time (not BlackBerry e-mails), more transparency and genuine dialogue. This in turn requires managers to prepare in advance and set regular feedback meetings with their professional groups. Given that both managers and the nomads will be on the move, this will present an even greater challenge.

At present it is estimated that nearly 47 per cent of all international assignments 'fail', with individuals deciding their career step is not only elsewhere but with another firm, typically a competitor. This is a huge waste of corporate investment. Probably a third of these 'resignations' could have been avoided by closer interest and dialogue between employer and the nomad as to the next move(s). Like most career management discussions, the trick is to identify the hooks of indecision or anxiety in career steps.

In many organizations, the problem is really one of ownership. Next-move discussions may not be best handled by immediate line managers but with a third party, a resourcing manager, a learning and development professional or as part of a wider, more transparent talent-review processes involving peer managers across functions and locations.

As organizations start to build more mobile workforces (directly or virtually), a number have recognized the need for a central section within HR to take responsibility for movements of initial 'global' graduates (I suggest taking the 10 per cent of the high potentials), the high performers with potential to be future leaders (the 5 per cent future talents) or the key international talents shaping markets abroad (1 per cent or 2 per cent market makers). Such a group should be on a half-yearly watch list. The goal should be to extend the organization tenure of this group by 20 per cent over the next three years. For example, ensuring proactive management of the initial graduate group raises their employment from three to five years, that of the mid-range high-potential professional from five to eight years, and that of the market shaper from eight to 12 years.

The employment brand is key to holding on to the nomads. Their drive for personal success is intrinsically linked to being part of a successful business unit. Just as a product brand aims to create a lasting image in the mind of a consumer, international organizations need to create an image which attracts talents with a promise of continual growth and learning. As our interviews have shown, this is even more heightened in the minds of the global nomads.

Second, the successful international employer needs to communicate a total employment relationship: highlighting what is truly valued and unique about what it is like to work in these markets, ie the *experience*. The Rio Tinto case study is a good example (see Part Five). For many of the young professionals now on the move, the package is less about benefits and more about sufficient pay (especially if tax-free) but only to raise the disposable income and not as a future saving plan, about lifestyle and career development, and about accessibility to leaders or senior coaches and early responsibility. These emerging market offices have a feel of pioneering spirits, flat hierarchies (if any!) and high intensity. As described, the work ethic is extraordinary and tends to blur into their social lives.

As Figure 12.4, from Mercer's 'What's Working?' survey[2], shows, the key dimensions of a new employment proposition are less about pay or benefits but more about respect of the people you work with, the type or challenge of work combined with career opportunities and flexibility of working arrangements. As the interviews noted, these are the core drivers of the global nomads.

The trade-off here is that the work environment is different. Firms can expect that there will be relationships within the office – as long as this is appropriate. Likewise, office hours will not be a strict 9 to 5 existence. In fact, it is more likely to be anything from 7 am to 10 pm to match customer needs. Corporate HQ needs to understand that part of the reason why these offices will outperform is not only the opportunity but also the extraordinary bonding and dedication to customers which occur.

There is also a need to widen diversity. Traditional expat programmes of the 1970s and 1980s were built on the assumption that US and European

FIGURE 12.4 What's working™ – what's important for employees?

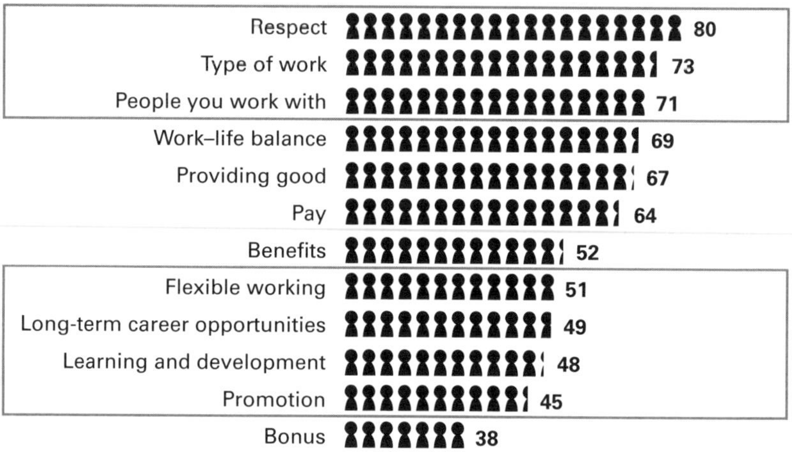

Respect	🚹🚹🚹🚹🚹🚹🚹🚹🚹🚹🚹🚹🚹🚹🚹🚹	80
Type of work	🚹🚹🚹🚹🚹🚹🚹🚹🚹🚹🚹🚹🚹🚹🚹	73
People you work with	🚹🚹🚹🚹🚹🚹🚹🚹🚹🚹🚹🚹🚹🚹🚹	71
Work–life balance	🚹🚹🚹🚹🚹🚹🚹🚹🚹🚹🚹🚹🚹🚹	69
Providing good	🚹🚹🚹🚹🚹🚹🚹🚹🚹🚹🚹🚹🚹🚹	67
Pay	🚹🚹🚹🚹🚹🚹🚹🚹🚹🚹🚹🚹🚹	64
Benefits	🚹🚹🚹🚹🚹🚹🚹🚹🚹🚹🚹	52
Flexible working	🚹🚹🚹🚹🚹🚹🚹🚹🚹🚹	51
Long-term career opportunities	🚹🚹🚹🚹🚹🚹🚹🚹🚹🚹	49
Learning and development	🚹🚹🚹🚹🚹🚹🚹🚹🚹🚹	48
Promotion	🚹🚹🚹🚹🚹🚹🚹🚹🚹	45
Bonus	🚹🚹🚹🚹🚹🚹🚹	38

© Mercer 2008

senior executives would be sent out to manage local offices, with most of the professional roles occupied by junior managers cutting their teeth in new surroundings. This was replaced by the idea of local offices managed by local managers with strategic or technical support from smaller selected expats (often recruited locally). This also proved problematic as many regions 'went native', following a local way of doing business inconsistent with the broader corporate machine.

Now in today's emerging world a different and more diverse model is appearing. The market leaders need global credibility and experience, with both management and operational teams more balanced between local talents and a more diverse group of nomads. The younger, local professionals are themselves more travelled, have broader mindsets and a thirst for new experiences. Thus the offices themselves are becoming more international. The nomads, both within region and from outside, are expecting all people within the office to be treated equally, without discriminatory pay ranges or benefit programmes. This is not always the norm in many of the emerging markets but this change will happen fast since neither the locals nor their international nomad colleagues will remain comfortable if these practices are continued.

In summary, multinational executives need to publicly recognize that the era of property wealth and share option growth is over in the mature markets. At present it is not quite clear what will replace it. Given the uncertainty, it is important that organizations stay close to their key talents and the high potentials driving their recovery – senior executives need to understand that their younger talents have a different set of financial and career constraints (eg the burden of student loans and cost of housing), which will drive rising levels of frustration. This is the time when senior leaders will need more heart than head and must stay close to their workforce.

References

1   Mercer's 2009 Expatriate Survey; www.mercer.com
2   Mercer's What's Working Survey; www.mercer.com

A winning formula

13

So as the dust clears after the global recession, we are witnessing different degrees of recovery and relative effects on global mobility, skills in demand, assignee duration and demographics. Latin American, Asian and European companies show the strongest increase in expatriates, as many of these companies are expanding overseas and searching for specific skills. Some multinational companies, however, have decreased the number of expatriates in favour of intra-regional moves.

Short-term and project-based assignments are on the rise due to project work, troubleshooting, critical skill shortages, cost pressures and family obligations.

Long-term assignments, those from one to three years, are getting shorter with a phasing out of allowances after three years and localization after a maximum of five years.

More nationalities are joining the mobility trend, and there is an increase in intra-regional transfers.

Family patterns are changing, with more dual income situations, more female assignees and increased single-status assignments.

Emerging-market multinationals have taken a leadership role in developing a breadth of talent for the global landscape. In India and China, students study in the West and return home for grooming within companies. Their development includes short-term assignments, continuous re-education and mentorship opportunities, whilst employers identify talent, employees' growth and skill trajectories. Tomorrow's leading players will likely have their roots in these rapidly growing, non-Western economies, but there is no guarantee they will stay. Organizations in emerging markets must now focus on retention, and must learn to view human capital management as more than data, compensation and peer competition. Many are digging deeper into talent management and issues of ROI, metrics and analytics – to not only retain this precious commodity but to also differentiate and define themselves as a firm with its own brand, identity and people planning. Emerging markets will continue to dominate worldwide growth with new entrants from Eastern Europe and the northern and southern tips of Africa. China and India will exhibit enough capacity and elasticity to continue their unprecedented growth, and state-owned enterprises in mining, IT and green technology will flex their global muscle.

Career development is playing a role in attracting the new global nomad

Given that one of the newest trends in global mobility is the emergence of a new kind of international assignee, organizations who look to this group to drive the future growth of international organizations will need to attract and hold on to them. We now know that a 'typical' global nomad:

- moves from assignment to assignment;
- has no home;
- can be utilized for rapid deployment wherever the need arises;
- is a non-traditional mobile employee;
- is 25 to 35 years old;
- is often multilingual;
- is adventurous and more motivated by challenges and travel than by pay.

Whilst the global nomad is a mystery to many in HR, whose attraction, retention and motivation programmes are based on sometimes outdated approaches, nomads, who rarely envision tenure longer than five years, place a high value on career development and a people-centred way of doing business in developing countries. They see their careers as a set of opportunities and experiences rather than a path of grade progression.

Organizations' craving for these high-potential individuals will only intensify, but companies are not sure how to attract and retain them. The following list serves as first steps to learning the language and culture of the elusive global nomad:

- Rethink career development. Where traditional HR programmes have been geared toward longevity, nomads have no intention of working for one organization longer than five years. Create ample opportunities for career development and encourage the greatest mobility for those who want to pursue it.
- Understand their psyche. A new employment model would strive to better understand these individuals and their desires for social networking, technology, travel opportunities, diverse work environments, open culture and an organization with a sincere, honest, global mindset.

- Flatten the organization. This new generation of mobile worker want to move away from hierarchies and vertical leadership to a people-centred culture of teamwork and lateral leadership. They seek greater internal and external networks in an organization with strong ethical values, one that is not based on tenure and that wants to make a difference.

- Engage. Today's younger, mobile worker may be electronically connected 15 or more hours per day, and modern modes of communication are vital. This goes beyond e-mail and includes face-to-face dialogue, internal social networks, buddy systems, approachable management and access to the highest levels.

Companies need to tackle the redeployment challenge

Today, repatriation has given way to redeployment, in which an organization identifies needed skills throughout the world and deploys high-potential employees (who view themselves as free agents) to where the needs are. When the staffing needs change, these expats are sent to the next assignment. This system is costly but allows an organization to effectively and rapidly staff a project and build important international experience in future senior managers.

Unfortunately, as many as half of all international assignments fail, defined as individuals who leave their assignments early, do not meet goals or return only to take a job with a competitor. When this happens, an organization's loss – financial and talent – is substantial. Companies need to rethink their approach to redeployment. Following are key questions to see if your organization is on the right track:

- Do we offer the same support – emotional and financial – when expats return as when they left? Transition home or to the next assignment can be even more difficult than the original assignment.

- Do we track what happens during and after assignments? A successful expat may be looking for the next challenge, and those who were successful before are more likely to be successful again – therefore identify, engage, retain and redeploy them. Additional information can be gleaned from the number of former assignees who have left the company, performance ratings before, during and after assignment, and surveys of current and former assignees.

- Are assignments 'real' or just opportunities to 'punch the career ticket?' Too often, headquarters identifies the next leaders, sends them overseas for their 'China experience', and they come back for promotion. Unclear and unfulfilled goals and incentives do not add value to the assignment or to the organization.

- Is there a plan and a talent strategy? Assignments based on real objectives should be planned in advance, continuously reviewed and seen as a series of tests for individuals with high potential.
- What is our return? Success cannot be determined without a clear picture of ROI and costs – overall, for high-potential assignees and others, and for those who leave the company.[1]

For global nomads, it is often not feasible or desirable to maintain home country coverage, as illustrated below. Most often the key purpose of international retirement programmes is to overcome barriers to utilizing home country or host country retirement programmes; they are generally not introduced as a means to provide unique provisions to a select group of employees.

It's time to create a global mobility manager

Perhaps no other HR role has changed as significantly in recent years as that of the global mobility manager. Once limited to bureaucratic duties and coordination, the expatriate programme manager has taken on added responsibilities and accountabilities.

The manager once relied on market data to support decisions around particular expatriate packages, and whilst this remains a critical element, there are now complex added dimensions. Today's global manager has been called upon to contain costs, enhance ROI and maximize the value of every assignment.

The new expatriate leader is a value chain manager responsible for identifying the best candidates for a particular assignment within a defined set of cost and value parameters. They must understand both the business imperative behind an assignment and work with line managers to ensure that the proper candidate is sourced, available and deployed as quickly as possible.

New expatriate managers must be:

- Business savvy. They must understand the people and the businesses they support, bring together diverse resources, emphasize strategy and supplying the right talent, and move beyond cost of living differential.
- Results oriented. They must ensure that the value and cost are specified, agreed and monitored so that performance deviations are identified, and if necessary, adjusted. They also have to make sure that the assigned talent positively contributes to the business well after assignment completion.
- Creative. The expatriate manager has to become an integrator and consultant and less of a bureaucrat and gatekeeper. For example, a

few years ago a multinational company sought to cut costs by issuing a blanket global decree that expats could no longer use company-funded drivers. A global mobility manager – thinking outside the box and anticipating possible adverse outcomes – would have realized that in some locations a driver was vital to expats as they often endured three- to four-hour commutes.

What's next? Business will become even more global, and demand for talented expatriates will grow. This promises tremendous value for a company that can be quicker, more strategic, creative and smarter than the competition. This begins with the new global mobility manager.[2]

We can therefore conclude that multinationals will need to strike a new employment proposition to attract, motivate and retain a winning share of these professionals.

A clear model is developing that involves far greater segmentation of expats into at least four different groups based on business need rather than contract length.

As Figure 13.1 demonstrates, multinationals can review their costs to match both the business and individual drives of the global nomads. As one major firm found following a review of the 3,500 people in its global mobile

FIGURE 13.1 Segmentation to determine primary purpose of mobility and cost containment

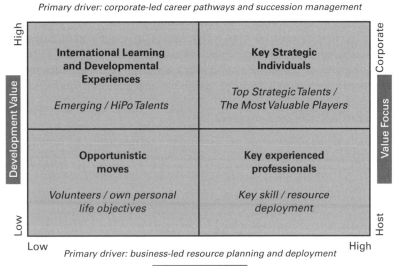

workforce, only 70 were in the strategic most valued player segment; about one thousand were either volunteers or targeted high potentials, leaving the vast majority in the new emerging class of global nomad professionals needed to execute business in the emerging markets.

The big win for all parties was a fundamental change in the programmes to more closely match individual international needs whilst saving the company over US$ 50 million in expat costs.

The second step is to look at globally mobility from a life cycle viewpoint for the nomad.

FIGURE 13.2 Managing the life cycle

Assignment identification	Candidate selection	Performance management	Talent management	Redeployment
Candidate identification	Deployment management		Succession planning	Separation

I would like to be an international talent	I want to accept an assignment	I've started my assignment	I'm part way through my assignment	I'm planning to return
What are the policy and criteria?	What will my reward package be?	How can I build my reputation and career whilst I'm here?	How can I keep in contact with my home office?	How successful have I been?
Do I qualify?	Will I have a job when it's completed?			What have I learned?
How do I find out more... who do I speak to?		Who will my mentor be?	How do I make sure I'm not losing touch with my previous friends and contacts?	How can I apply my new skills in my home office?
What support would the company give me?	When can I meet my new colleagues?	How can I make sure I'm learning new skills?		What sort of role do I want?
	Who will help me with the practical matters if it involves a move? removals... choosing a house... choosing a school... financial matters?	What are my goals and objectives?	Who is managing the business / doing 'my job' whilst I'm not there?	What's available
What are the logistics?				How has my view of the world changed whilst I've been away?
How would my family be affected?		How do I and my family make new friends and contacts?	What changes are happening in my home office?	

© Mercer 2010[4]

The idea of assignment life cycle is an interesting concept for both the company and the nomad. First, it implies there are phases when there needs to be dialogue about how the initial transfer has gone (remarkably, one-way employee traffic here!), degree of family integration, progress and success in role, next moves, country transfer or repatriation. And this needs to take place much earlier than most firms really think. The trick is to place hooks into the nomad mindset to catch the 'next wave' before it breaks. Typically this can be six, 14, 24 or 33 months into the relevant contract to ensure that a conversation in respect of future intentions is had, and that the individual feels valued and that their options have been noted.

Finally, there is one other major consideration to take account of as the world embraces an ever-expanding global workforce: the partner's viewpoint. Though the partner may be male or female, the majority are still female. This viewpoint will therefore be far better covered in a journal currently being written: *A Year in the Life of a Nomad's Wife*!

References

1 'Global Mobility', Thomas P Flannery and Michael Piker, *Benefits & Compensation International*, 1 July 2010
2 Ibid
3 'Global Mobility', Jim Matthewman, *Benefits & Compensation International*, 1 July 2009, pp 21–25
4 'Mobility in the Middle East – Roundtable Discussion', Jim Matthewman, 24 November 2009

PART FIVE
How do multinationals envision mobility and the future workforce?

Introduction

Given the phenomenal change happening across the world plus the demographic and generational issues highlighted in Parts Two and Three, how do CEOs and senior HR leaders see the future workforce? How much change are they predicting? What are the critical roles and key skills that will be needed in 2015 and 2020? How mobile do they expect the workforce to be? How will they attract, motivate and retain Generation Y?

These questions were put to 12 leaders of major multinationals across the world. I am very grateful to them for their candid insights.

A view to the future

14

12 corporate perspectives

Dr Nasser Mareth, Group CEO, Qtel International

Qtel International (QI), formerly Qatar Telecom, has grown rapidly in the past three years to become an integrated telecom operator with a business presence in 17 countries. This transformational growth has been spectacular, with subscribers growing from 0.5 million in 2005 to 1.7 million in 2007 and 53.4 million in 2009; revenues have risen from 644 million Qatari Riyals in 2005 to 4.8 billion in 2009.

The group's vision is to be among the top 20 telecommunication companies by 2020. Its strategy is focused on three business segments: consumer business, consumer broadband and consumer managed services in three geographical regions – Middle East, Asian subcontinent and Asia-Pacific. Of note, the organization has decided that Africa remains difficult, expensive and too fragmented at present. Dr Nasser says: 'Asian countries are considered more stable but require more process and revised leadership systems.'

The group's path to growth has seen acquisitions in Oman, Iraq, the Philippines, Laos, Cambodia, Singapore, Indonesia, Maldives, Saudi Arabia, Palestine, Algeria, Tunisia and Kuwait. Whilst the growth continues to deliver double-digit growth in revenue, EBITDA and net profit, the journey of growth has been different from that of other competitors. QI has a diversified portfolio: 75 per cent of its revenues come from outside Qatar with a good mix of growth from emerging and mature markets. It holds number one or number two positions in each of its chosen markets and these positions are growing in North Africa and Asia. Growth is also continuing in Qatar despite strong competition. In the latter, data and added value services have been the growth drivers.

Dr Nasser believes success has come from strong management capabilities which have applied discipline in executing strategy with a focus on operational efficiency. In particular, QI has applied effective post-acquisition implementation plans focused on value.

But there are key challenges within the telecom industry. In certain markets mobile penetration is reaching saturation level, compounded by increasing competition and new players. All this, of course, is within a variety of regulatory regimes and fast-changing economic change around the globe. In the next five years Dr Nasser anticipates new entrants into their markets, especially from the entertainment and IT industries (Google, Microsoft and Apple), and these will start to converge with the telecom providers. The mature markets (in QI's case the Middle Eastern states) will see further consolidation of firms. This will, however, mean that data and added-value services will continue to rise given the Gulf Cooperation Council nations' good basic mobile infrastructure, but such moves will also put a greater emphasis on efficiency and cost optimization – difficult where states have strong nationalization targets. Hence the higher growth will come from Asian operations.

Technology and mobile content will advance rapidly – the telecom providers own part of the future solution and the key will be who owns the content. New partnerships will evolve but need regulators to recognize this changing face of the markets and the investments already made.

From an employer perspective the expansion has meant that the organization now has over 20,000 employees, of whom the original home market makes up only 2,500. The technology will standardize and in the future will no longer be a major differentiator for service quality. As quality is standardized, there will be growing opportunities to outsource these areas. This means that the workforce will shift in composition from an emphasis on technical skills to marketing, business development and customer service operations. The new workforce will focus on individuals who have superior skills and knowledge of local markets, are commercially minded and able to create partnerships and relationships with third parties.

Customization of packages and services to local markets will be really important, so local knowledge will be at a premium. There will be less centralized management as speed to market will demand decisions at source. Group functions will need to concentrate on cost optimization and common platforms, process and systems in the business and support functions such as finance and HR. Strategy and marketing functions at the group level will need to be at the top of their fields to stay ahead of the game, building universal partnerships with multiple customers and suppliers.

The formation of the Qtel International Group has created opportunities by offering up new challenges in multiple disciplines. Originally the parent Qatar Telecom was not seen by young Qataris as an employer of choice but with international expansion this is changing. Part of the reason for this is that there has been a growth in private international schools within Qatar and this has opened the eyes and raised the ambition of Qatari youth. The organization is establishing a new programme of international mobility and the company is also actively recruiting professionals from known migratory locations such as Lebanon and Japan. The biggest minefield for the future workforce will be how to ensure effective knowledge sharing across the organization.

Pekka Lundmark, CEO, Konecranes

Konecranes is a Finnish world-leading 'lifting business' organization serving a broad range of customers, including manufacturing and process industries, shipyards, ports and terminals. Its productivity-enhancing lifting solutions combine lifting equipment and services. It currently employs some 9,700 people in 485 locations in some 43 countries. Its main spheres of operation are the USA, Germany, France and the UK, but over the past five years there has been a marked shift towards the Far East, especially China. Over a third of its revenue now comes from non-OECD operations. The company's vision is to reach a global market share of 30 per cent.

Whilst the long-term outlook remains positive, the organization has had to deal with uncertainty in the market and price erosion, and therefore adjust its overall cost base. Its key clients are trying to globalize and rationalize their relationships with suppliers.

The company is seeing a clear difference in trends between the developed and emerging markets. In the former there is a strong focus on productivity improvements, coupled with rising environmental awareness driving demand for better technology, automation and systems. Customer organizations are shifting their production to more cost-competitive regions and outsourcing non-core operations such as maintenance. It expects orders to stabilize in service and standard lifting, although the heavy lifting category (typically industries handling heavy loads: ports, shipyards and bulk material terminals) is expected to fluctuate. Price erosion will be more acute in new equipment areas, so in the immediate term preserving customer relationships is critical.

The company is adjusting its workforce to reflect the shift in focus of demand – at present about 2,000 are employed in the USA, 1,000 in Germany, but over the next year the number in China will rise from 800 to 1,300. The number of expats is relatively low (about 50) but there is an increasing group of technical professionals being employed as operational specialists on localized contracts or short-term assignments.

Mr Lundmark expects 'a strong shift to China, India, Russia, the Middle East and Latin America (Brazil) in the next few years (less than five), although expansion to Africa will take longer (between five and 10 years). For each of these areas the organization needs local talent and this will probably come through acquisitions since organic growth is too slow'.

One of the major challenges in talent management is the issue of knowledge transfer. Technical skills can be identified and developed reasonably quickly; the main issue will be leadership capability. The organization needs to find suitable candidates with entrepreneurial global mindsets who can not only deliver locally but build larger customer relationships. The emphasis will be on business development and customer retention in the next five years.

The future workforce will need broader professional skill sets so that it adds more value and takes on bigger roles. Service engineers will be expected to spot opportunities for add-on business, not simply the delivery of spare parts (as of today). The company is expecting the technical/professional teams to take on more responsibility and become the 'eyes and ears' of the organization.

The workforce will need to change. At present the organization has many staff aged between 50 and 65 and there is a gap emerging with the under-40s. The organization needs to shift its people strategy to focus on the latter group as these will fuel future growth. Mr Lundmark can see a big difference between the generations, especially those aged under 30. This younger talent pool needs more systematic career paths and new skill sets. He senses that they have less commitment and more time will need to be devoted to managing this group. The issue is that this talent pool is potentially more competent than those managing them (Generation X), giving a rising leadership problem.

Dr Tim Miller, Director Property, Research and Assurance, Standard Chartered plc, and Chairman, Standard Chartered Korea

Standard Chartered plc is one of the major international banks. Whilst being registered in the UK, it has grown from its roots in Hong Kong and Singapore to now lead the way in the developing countries of Asia, Africa and the Middle East. Unlike other major international banks, Standard Chartered was less exposed to the financial crisis. Its half-year results for the first two quarters of 2009 reflect its strength, with profit before taxation rising by 10 per cent to US$2.84 billion; income was up by 14 per cent to US$7.69 billion and total assets rose to US$411 billion. So even during the testing times, the bank has been able to maintain strong performance through disciplined management and cost controls but also through the diversity of the business and the markets of the East. It prides itself on deep local heritages and a very strong set of shared values. Sustainable economic profit is dependent on the sustainability of the communities it serves.

Tim Miller notes that the World Bank has predicted that the rise of the Eastern economies will eclipse the recovery of OECD countries in the next five years. The impact on bank operations is quite simply 'more of the same'.

The organization has always used a relatively high proportion of expats throughout the world, drawn from the 100-plus nationalities working at the bank. In the main the bank looks to use local country management teams supported by specialists. The bank has striven to implement a high degree of diversity throughout the business and this is reflected on the board. Unlike many competitors, Standard Chartered is able to offer young professionals real long-term career opportunities full of variety by the very nature of the organization's range of business and its focus on developing markets. The flow of talent will reflect the rising importance of the East in the next three to five years as the organization looks to build out the long-term careers of rising high potentials from China, Korea and India to other operating locations. Such aims are challenging, especially for female executives from certain countries where the social infrastructure is very strong but significantly weaker in other countries. Likewise, the Middle East, where nationalization targets often mean locals are placed in 'easy, comfortable' positions early in careers makes it hard to offer career growth unless the individual is prepared to move.

Dr Miller does not expect the bank's overall business model to change much in light of the recovery as this has held the organization in good stead for the past 10-plus years. What he expects to see is that local presence will deepen and expand where this is appropriate to match business opportunities; for example, in Saudi Arabia. In Standard Chartered's terms, 'global' does not necessarily mean big. What is more important is to have sufficient scale in chosen local markets. Brazil is a case in point, where it will be important to have decent market share given the changing landscape and rising trade with Asia and China in particular.

Over the next five to 10 years, Dr Miller believes 'that the key skill sets of tomorrow will still be the same as today but the matrix organization environment will require changing behaviour and a changing mindset. Increasingly individuals will need to adapt to working across different time zones to seek out consensus with colleagues from different businesses, different functions and different locations. Whilst in the past individuals would always reference back to their country market base, now everyone has to be international. The organization will feel much more like a federation of international businesses. We are shamelessly looking to copy best practices from other organizations to understand how to manage across boundaries.'

Today the organization has about 70,000 employees; about 1 per cent (ie 800) are expats. About 10 to 15 per cent are in professional and management grades. In the future the bank will expect a large number of these to be mobile. Two-thirds of graduates entering the business will be offered short-term assignments within two years. The company has a priority to exchange talent across borders but these high potentials are actioned only where there is a clear business need. A major challenge for the future is response times. These have been changed completely by aggressive technology. Dr Miller says: 'Today's BlackBerry means that individuals are pressurized into providing instant response at any hour of the day. However, swift decisions do not necessarily equate to right decisions – individuals will need new skills, requiring business maturity. Poor decisions taken locally could have significant global impact. Tomorrow's workforce will need a greater sense of personal ownership and innovation. Managers will be more entrepreneurial, will be asked to weigh the impact of decisions and take accountability.'

The organization will need to agree a new purpose, vision and values that have higher resonance with business leaders as these individuals will have more responsibility in transmitting these principles with more calm and sincerity than before. Dr Miller states that, 'given the crises and upheaval, employees need leaders to provide a new moral compass to help others through. In particular, this needs to help provide others with clarity around roles and their contributions.'

Generation Y offer new skills, new vibrancy and new perspectives. Dr Miller sees Generation Y as being more choosy about their employers, especially in respect to the world around them. They are expecting clear corporate statements about the firm's position on the environment, business ethics and on tackling discrimination. They come with a global mindset by using the technology to access specific areas of the world. In his view they do not need to managed differently but they do need more of the basics. Standard Chartered believes the key is effective engagement of all staff. Dr Miller states that this can be achieved by:

- providing clarity in what individuals are being asked to do;
- ensuring they have the tools they need;
- providing honest and regular feedback;
- being clear as to how the organization is going to look after them.

Shaikh Ahmed Al Khalifa, Group General Manager, HR and Development, Batelco Group

In a few years Batelco (Bahrain Telecom) has evolved from a national company providing fixed services to some half a million of Bahrain's residents into a diversified telecom operator in seven countries with over 5 million subscribers. In Bahrain it has the leading market share of fixed line, mobile and broadband; in Jordan it is the number two operator of similar services through Umniah; in Yemen it is the number one mobile provider; in Kuwait the number one broadband operator; it has invested in wi-max through Etihad Atheeb Telecom in Saudi Arabia, and data services in Egypt and most recently in mobile communications in India. In 2008 total income was some 319 million BHD (Bahraini dinars) with profits of 104 million BHD.

Batelco has recognized that its people strategy needs to change. Until recently the current structure was largely one of senior Bahrainis and expats occupying executive and senior management positions with qualified technicians, engineers and customer service staff drawn from local or nearby countries. With the creation of a group operating model and increased competition within Bahrain and the Gulf region, there was little proactive management of key talents and a leadership succession pipeline. With new technology offerings, the senior management has invested heavily in creating a Learning and Development Academy, a systematic talent management approach backed up by web-based software, classroom and e-learning initiatives. This was partly to address perceived lack of development and career management and secondly a growing need to create a mobile executive and senior management team capable of maximizing the integration and execution of its ambitious international growth strategy.

The evolution into a group model has also highlighted generational differences in the workforce. Shaikh Khalifa says: 'Managing today's workforce is different; in the past the relatively stable organization models have changed to reflect different heritages and operational priorities. This means the size, shape and format need to be flexible and adaptable. Career paths have changed – today's 25-year-old is expected to experience anywhere from three to five careers in a lifetime. Traditionally many working at the company had very long tenure, and in many cases Bahrain Telecom had been their only employer.'

Batelco also recognized that it had the combination of Traditionalists, Baby Boomers, Generation X and Generation Y employees that I have described in previous chapters. Given the learning and development brief of Shaikh Khalifa's role, he has also noticed a difference in learning needs and learning styles in each of the workforce generations, as illustrated in Table 14.1.

So the challenge as Shaikh Khalifa sees it, 'is that age diversity has increased the complexity in recruiting, training and motivating workers and the big question is whether HR professionals can satisfy all the generations working together in the same workplace and at the same time reap the benefits of their unique experiences and learn the new skills required by the company'.

Inevitable talent shortages will appear as economies recover, so it will be important that all generations achieve their potential – not just Generation Y. Given the different learning and varied communication styles highlighted above, this will require flexible learning and development approaches. All this is happening at a time when training budgets and training staff numbers are being significantly reduced. This will force organizations such as Batelco to cut out non-strategic training, to rely on webcasting and virtual

TABLE 14.1 Traditionalists, Baby Boomers, Generation X and Generation Y

Demographic Group	Year Born (age range)	Values, Traits, Characteristics	Learning Styles
Traditionalists	1928–1945 (65+ years old)	Hierarchical, loyal to institution, motivated by financial rewards and security	Traditional, instructor-led, reading, homework **'teach me'**
Baby Boomers	1946–1964 (46–64 years old)	Idealistic, competitive, striving to achieve	Traditional, group effort, expert-driven, self-driven **'lead me to information'**
Generation X	1965–1980 (30–45 years old)	Self-reliant, willing to change rules, tribal and community orientated	Team-driven, collaborative, 'wisdom of crowds', peer-to-peer **'connect me to people'**
Generation Y	1981–2000 (10–29 years old)	Confident, impatient, socially conscious, family-centric, tech savvy, customized	Give context and meaning, make it fun, search and explore, entertain me **'connect me to everything'**

classrooms and make best use of what it has got. In particular, Shaikh Khalifa sees a move to more informal learning and rapid e-learning tools.

Batelco has therefore adopted what is known as 'blended learning' – a mix of classroom training and online learning. Mandatory or compliance training is nearly all completed online as it is easy to deploy, measure and report. But for the rest, organizations need to consider different delivery mechanisms by using audio, mobile and collaborative environments – this is especially true of younger generations in the workplace.

The organization has recently embarked on a programme based on the Skillsoft Learning Growth Model™. This has five levels:

Supplementary level: to 'initiate learning' by introducing scalable learning resources into Batelco.

Target level: to 'manage learning' by expanding the overall content, the use of resources and features.

Strategic level: to 'align learning' by linking the learning content to the key competencies and critical job roles.

Systematic level: to 'integrate learning' by linking learning to performance goals and organizational value.

Optimize level: to create 'enterprise-wide learning' to ensure skill levels maintain organizational advantage.

This strategy, underpinned by Microsoft's e-Learning, aims to develop an organization with a culture where self-learning is encouraged and the tools are readily available. In 2005, 60 volunteers opted for a pilot; by 2009 over 250 different courses were available with over 540 courses completed.

This fresh view of learning and development not only plays well to the generational mix at Batelco Group, it also allows participation from an increasingly, mobile workforce.

David Haines, CEO, Grohe AG

Grohe AG is Europe's largest and the world's leading single-brand manufacturer and supplier of sanitary fittings – holding about 8 per cent of the world market. Its aim is to set the standard for quality, technology and design to deliver the perfect flow of water. It operates in over 200 markets around the world with six production plants – three in Germany, one in Portugal, one in Thailand and one in Canada.

The company was established in 1936 by Friedrich Grohe in the German city of Hemer. In the 1930s bathrooms were considered modest areas but in the post-war boom they became key with the introduction of gas and electric water boilers. By 1980 people were prepared to experiment with colours and hence design and fashion.

In the last few years, Grohe has seen significant growth both in the mature markets as personal consumers and corporate clients look to refurbish or renovate existing properties with latest design with green, environmental credentials whilst the developing and emerging markets offer new-build and state-of-the-art smart technology.

Mr Haines says: 'Our strategy is clear – we anticipate positive single-digit growth in the mature markets as individuals seek betterment in personal well-being with a strong environmental basis, with double-digit growth in the developing and emerging markets in China and India but not forgetting Brazil and Africa.'

Whilst the last two years have been challenging, Grohe has also seen the downturn as an opportunity to take market share by focusing on brand, business development and sales. With a change of ownership from family to international institutions, a major restructuring saw the workforce halved and nearly all the former senior management replaced. A new strategy focused on reinforcing brand saw a shift in the workforce from predominately manufacturing to a better mix of technologists and sales and marketing.

'We needed a new mindset based on unconditional delivery – an attitude that individuals will still deliver come what may. The new management were selected on the basis of ambition, global mindset and team orientation.'

A generational shift occurred with the average age of the workforce reduced by 10 years, with most managers now in their 40s or 30s. Mr Haines believes that Grohe is attracting more Generation Y professionals for the following reasons:

- The organization is operating in a global industry with one of the world's most precious resources. Its slogan is 'Enjoy water.'
- It has strong brand presence in both mature and emerging markets.
- Grohe is a mid-size company – big enough to offer challenging opportunities yet small enough to remain personal.
- It is entrepreneurial, agile, offers responsibility and is run as a meritocracy.

Whilst positioning the organization as a global firm, the shift in economic markets has meant that many former global positions have been replaced by regional general managers. The headquarters have also been moved to make recruitment and retention more attractive.

In the future the organization will look to attract the best from the world's top 50 consumer firms and, given the opportunities, mindset and multicultural requirements described above, these people by definition will be the global nomads. In tomorrow's world, decisions will be made closer to the consumer. As Mr Haines says, 'You cannot run Asia from Germany!'

Brian Schipper, Global Head of HR, Cisco Systems

Networking is the essential connective tissue of modern communications, commerce and life's experiences. Without IP networking, today's IT, telecommunications and entertainment industries would be smaller, siloed and less significant. This is transforming life around the world because networking technology connects us all and breaks down barriers to human progress.

Cisco is only 26 years old. Since the company's inception, Cisco engineers have been leaders in the development of Internet Protocol (IP)-based networking technologies. Today, with 65,000 employees worldwide, this tradition of innovation continues with industry-leading products and solutions in the company's core development areas of routing and switching, as well as in advanced technologies. Today the organization generates some US$40 billion in revenue.

As the leader in this world-changing technology, Cisco's vision is 'Changing the way we work, live, play and learn'. This is bigger and more important than the internet, productivity or communications. Cisco has evolved and is now building the next generation company. In the past its business was primarily around transactions between people and machines; under Cisco 2.0 it foresees interactions that are person to person through the use of intelligent information networks: from point products to process solutions. It's about transforming human experiences and furthering human progress. This is a much broader and bolder aspiration than Cisco has ever tried before, but no other company can claim this: 'All Cisco employees wear a badge to remind them of our mission and our corporate culture. Ultimately, our culture boils down to one critical idea: a focus on our customer's success.'

Today, Cisco has a global workforce, with technology centres located broadly (for example in the USA, Canada, UK, Belgium, Israel, United Arab Emirates, India, China, Singapore and Australia) to access engineering talent throughout the world. Cisco's global employee population is divided generally equally, with about one-third of employees in engineering, about one-third in sales, and about one-third spread across the remaining disciplines. It has a mix of generations, although the average age of employees is just over 38 years, with average tenure of 4.6 years. This workforce profile reflects Cisco's intense focus on delivering the right technology solutions to meet customers' needs. And because Cisco uses these same technology solutions to run its own business, Cisco has been better able to satisfy customers in new ways, drive collaboration across its global organization, and deliver ongoing productivity gains for shareholders.

In October 2007 Cisco unveiled its state-of-the-art Globalization Centre, East Campus in Bangalore as part of its overall US$1.1 billion investment plan for India. The facility houses an advanced Global Briefing Centre to showcase Cisco's latest technology solutions and provide an environment for closer collaboration with partners in spotlighting solutions for customers in emerging markets such as India, China, the Middle East, Africa, Asia and Latin America. The campus also houses the largest campus data centre outside the USA and will provide a focal point for demonstrating next-generation virtualization technologies and service-oriented network architectures that support customers' global environments.

Mr Schipper states that 'India is at the heart of our globalization vision and provides a platform for Cisco to capitalize on the growth potential and lead market transitions in the emerging world. The commitment we are making to truly globalize our business is reflective of the changing business models of our customers and partners.'

Part of the reason for choosing Chennai as its eastern base – known affectionately internally as 'The Kitchen', the place for dreaming up recipes – was the country's political democracy, a judicial system which would protect the company's intellectual property, and the source of the fastest-growing young population in the world. Indeed, Cisco claims that '70 per cent of the world's population is within reach on a five-hour flight. So the proximity of India as a place for globalization is a fantastic opportunity to capitalize on the talent opportunities of the region. To make this real, we have pledged that 20 per cent of our top talent will be based in India. So we build out an organization of 10,000 people, we're talking about 1,000 managers, we're talking about 200 to 250 directors, and a minimum of 50 VPs.

'Our observations are that in India the younger generation is acquiring higher levels of education; the workforce is highly mobile (last decade, more than a third of the Indian workforce migrated), is eager to learn and has a high willingness to solve problems. Whilst Cisco's brand image is a great recruiting tool for attracting new talent, it does not retain. Therefore we need to be competitive and create development and career opportunities.'

Part of the new employment proposition is that Cisco engages in highly challenging work through 'mega-projects'. These are a phenomenon stemming from global trends such as urbanization and the creation of middle-class populations. A new era of wealth is being established in some regions, such as the Arabian Gulf where rising oil prices are funding countrywide development projects – for example, large technology service providers building out infrastructure in emerging countries and regions, grand-scale real-estate development projects and planned 'smart cities' or government-driven regional deployments of infrastructure in emerging markets (in Saudi, United Arab Emirates, Qatar, Azerbaijan and Singapore.

'This growth is spurring on a new organization and decision-making design based on an entirely different level of collaboration enabled by networked Web 2.0 technologies. The result is formalized social networking groups where business process and the right networked Web 2.0 technologies have been applied. It enables teams to move and make decisions with a tremendous amount of speed and agility. Cross-functional coordination is the real key to their success, but it will also require a new way of doing business. I believe that what we are attempting to do is define what organizations of the future look like.'

One example that Cisco uses is one of its innovative and collaborative technologies – TelePresence. The objective was to address several challenges facing businesses today, including ineffective remote meetings, the increasing demand for collaboration, global business operations and the need to access highly distributed subject-matter expertise. Traditional videoconferencing never met expectations, falling considerably short in the areas of quality, simplicity and reliability. From the beginning, Cisco's focus was on experience. Its TelePresence range offers a suite of real-time, virtual meeting solutions that enable more interactions with the right people at the right time – allowing you not just to meet, but to connect in a way never before possible.

Cathy Turner, Group Human Resources Director, Barclays Bank plc

Barclays is a major global financial services provider engaged in retail banking, credit cards, corporate banking, investment banking and investment management services, with an extensive international presence in Europe, the Americas, Africa and Asia. The company operates in more than 50 countries and employs more than 145,000 people serving over 49 million customers worldwide. It has a heritage of over 300 years of success.

John Varley, Group Chief Executive, has set out a consistent strategic direction based on achieving 'good growth through time by diversifying our business base and increasing our presence in markets and segments that are growing rapidly'. This is reflected in the company's revenue whereby over 51 per cent is attributed to regions other than the UK. For many, there is a surprise that UK retail banking contributes only 13 per cent of income (2009 interim results) compared with some 17 per cent from emerging markets and nearly 40 per cent from Barclays Capital, its investment banking arm.

Barclays has weathered the recession better than most and indeed has been opportunistic in building its investment banking by buying key parts of Lehman Brothers within a week of the financial crisis brought on by the collapse of the American investment bank. It has managed the impact of the credit crunch whilst still maintaining its strategic momentum by remaining outside significant government investment. In 2009 it recorded over £16 billion turnover (an increase of 37 per cent over 2008) with profit before tax up by 8 per cent to nearly £3 billion.

Significantly, Barclays emerging markets division, with operations in 14 countries in India, the Middle East, Africa, Pakistan and Indonesia, has over 18,000 employees with over £7.7 billion in customer accounts (about 80 per cent of the UK total), with approximately 40 per cent of the UK workforce and half the distribution points/branches.

Sustainability has become its mantra – proving to be carbon neutral across Europe in 2009; it achieved platinum rating in the Community Corporate Responsibility Index and ranked joint first in the UK government's Carbon Disclosure Project.

Cathy Turner comments: 'This is an interesting time when key moments will shape history – Barclays has not sought government aid, yet still it is still able to deliver profits and is in good shape. Actually we are stronger, we have learned a lot because the crisis (or any downturn) tests systems under stress. At present we feel we have got more right than wrong'.

There has been a massive change, with the subprime crisis proving to be the tipping point for the whole financial services industry. 'What is happening now is that business models in the industry are being reshaped but it will take time. Given national government's response, there are huge changes being discussed and planned in terms of policy and systems to be in place by 2020.'

Most significantly, regulation has now become the number one priority to ensure consistency and professionalism in a climate of risk aversion. There are major interplays at work involving governments, central banks and private banking firms, all of which are being asked to join up and step up to avoid the overreaction previously seen in Japan.

So what is the impact for Barclays? First, there is now a question mark around whether 'universal banking' (ie providing the full range of investment banking, corporate, private, retail and commercial banking) is acceptable in the new post-Lehman world. Ms Turner says: 'Most people will not know that Barclays investment banking arm has grown significantly with the part assimilation of Lehman Brothers business. However, Barclays is not shifting its business from West to East. The organization has been investing there over many years, taking advantage of opportunistic deals.'

In respect of the future workforce, Ms Turner notes that huge amounts of time are being absorbed in the tactical reactions to the medium- and longer-term implications of the regulatory change. But she is convinced that this will drive a new wave of innovation to create tomorrow's shareholder value.

'But in the new world, stakeholder value will emphasize sustainable value, the world economy and a need to rebuild trust. This means that the multinationals across the world which offered a 'career proposition based on 20 years' loyalty' will need a serious rethink.'

Ms Turner expects the employment model to change – Barclays will still seek out the same level of commitment but there will no longer be a single set of characteristics or a one-size employment proposition. Instead she expects a number of different types of workers – some whom the bank will want to keep for 15 years and some specialists for up to five years.

'The future world will be less coherent: emotional needs will figure highly but larger multinationals will still need systems and processes, especially in the new regulatory environment. These companies will need to be more multicultural to encourage cross-border business to mirror the world's new customer base. This means staff will have to be more mobile.'

Hugh Bucknall, Chairman, Singapore Offshore Services

Singapore Offshore Services (SOS) is typical of the new wave of organizations taking advantage of the shift in trade from West to East. In five years the company, which grew out of some initial work in India and Jordan, has grown at 200 per cent and sees this trend rising as a sense of urgency is driving more European blue chips to look for a professional outsourcing one-shop solution. Singapore was an easy choice to set up as a headquarters, whilst Vietnam provides low infrastructure cost. SOS became the first organization to offer outsourcing services in Vietnam and has benefited from significant concessions as a first mover.

SOS embodies a new opportunist firm combining consulting, offshoring and outsourcing. It is hungry and ambitious. The market is clearly big and growing, with substantial interest from the USA, Japan and India tapping into a need to address customer needs ranging from cost effectiveness, talent shortages, constrained growth, a need to focus on core business, struggling to collect cash but lacking local know-how and quality to eliminate inefficiencies and errors.

But a key insight into these new competitors to the multinational giants is the company's strategy: 'to perfect the model, stay below the radar and to hunt in virgin territory and to consolidate success before global visibility'. The organization uses internet v2.0 web-based surveys to glean local knowledge to match client needs, highlight market hotspots and respond with agility. This is a challenge for most multinationals.

Using Singapore as a corporate base allows the company to provide entrepreneurial advice across the breadth of Asia, whilst its Vietnamese outsourcing centre provides added-value back-office support beyond order and accounts receivable services. The organization now provides system analysis, client management, project management and CRM selling as integrated services, with overall client satisfaction at the heart of operations. The organization's clients include major European financial services organizations, German manufacturers, Asian retailers.

This has meant the operations have switched from cost reduction to focus on attention to detail, operational excellence. The staffing of the support centre uses a combination of talented locals and experienced expats. The Vietnamese are highly numerate, speak French and English to a very high level, and also Japanese and Korean. The talent has an extremely high level of professional education. This means staff are able to apply significant added value to even the most routine analysis, so the solution is more than report generation – it will include trend analysis, profitability and currency opportunities.

As India starts to overheat and total remuneration costs rise, Vietnam and Cambodia await. The latter is not quite ready yet but SOS believes its Mekong Delta experience provides an excellent launch pad as the next wave comes through with the growing recovery.

Mr Bucknall believes that 'the next five years will continue to show strong growth as organizations look east and they see the insatiable appetite of the new emerging markets. The UK, USA and Australia are looking at Singapore, Vietnam and Cambodia with keen interest. But equal interest is not coming from India as the outsourcers start to look to outsource or subcontract their own work; Japan and Korea are also actively seeking opportunities.'

He states that 'the new generation workforce (today's 22- to 28-year-olds) will be more similar to the Baby Boomers of the late 1960s and will hop from job to job for two or three years but then many will look for more stability as they take on more personal responsibilities. But there is a difference. Generation Y does need pandering to. They are more tech savvy, have high expectations of both experience and reward. In the long run they will make better middle managers because they have a greater appreciation of diversity and multiculturalism. They also recognize that the local workforces in the emerging markets are as smart, work harder and are keener than in the past. Hence jobs (and talent) will also follow the flow to the East.'

His advice is that organizations should not try and fit the trend but actively plan for it and take advantage of the nomadic cities like Dubai and Tokyo as training posts.

Beryl Cook, Executive Vice President, News Corporation International

News Corporation is a diversified global media company with operations in a number of industry segments including filmed entertainment, television, cable network programming, direct broadcast satellite television, integrated marketing services, newspapers and information services, and book publishing. The company has a market capitalization of approximately US$37 billion, and operates in more than 60 countries, principally the USA, continental Europe, the UK, Australia, Asia and Latin America.

The company began with one newspaper in Adelaide, Australia, but today has more than 250 properties covering the creation, packaging and distribution of content ranging from news to sport and entertainment. Businesses range from newspapers and book publishing, to pay and free television, and social networking.

The News Corporation workforce has over 50,000 employees globally.

As a diversified, truly international business with a spread of businesses covering varied genres, platforms and markets, News Corp has been overall largely insulated from economic pressures in any particular market. However, the global recession was widespread, and in 2009 the company reported a decline in operating income to US$3.6 billion, US$1.7 billion down on the previous year's record of US$5.3 billion, and revenues of US$30 billion – down 8 per cent on the previous year.

However, all businesses balanced an aggressive programme of cost cutting with continued investment in core opportunities and digital development, and in the most recent quarterly results (for fourth quarter ended December 2009) reported revenue growth of 10 per cent to US$8.7 billion.

Recent investments include 9.09 per cent stake in Rotana Group, the Middle East media group, and an increased stake of 45 per cent in pay television operator Sky Deutschland in Germany.

The company is almost 60 years old, and has continued a pattern of launching or acquiring new businesses almost every six months. Acquisitions tend to be opportunities to expand the company's reach or diversity of content, or ways to create value or leverage.

The brands within News Corp, such as Fox, *The Times*, *Wall Street Journal*, MySpace and HarperCollins, are strong business and product brands in their own right – and in any cases are stronger employer brands than News Corp. For new or developing businesses there is usually a stronger desire to leverage the News Corp employer brand. One challenge is to communicate that the company has 'a brand within News Corp for everyone', that it offers a wide range of career opportunities across the world.

This has stemmed from management's belief in a decentralized business model where CEOs are chosen and expected to run and grow their business. There are, however, some strong cultural values that the businesses share including a restless drive to improve, to do things better, and be the best, the leader and pacesetter in what they do. The journalistic foundations of the company set a pattern of challenging the status quo, defying critics and the 'way things are done', and a focus on informing and entertaining consumers in ways that connect, inspire and often incite reaction.

News Corp has been active in international markets including Europe and Asia for more than two decades, with over 30,000 employees based outside the USA, so the company sees itself as a global company or a federation of businesses, rather than a centralized corporate or a US company with overseas outposts.

The decentralized approach to the business and a belief in taking News Corp's expertise and investment but developing very localized businesses and products means the number of expatriates has been relatively small – except for small teams of specialists including nomads, posted in for launches and relaunches.

Specialists develop skills and products, and nomads develop skills, products and strategy, and infuse culture and behaviours.

Each year, just over 300 employees move between businesses, including about 100 who move between countries. A smaller number are widely viewed as nomads, who have a track record of successive moves to varied markets. News Corp also has a secondment programme through which employees can go and work in other businesses for up to five months. In addition, News Corp's businesses between them hire thousands of interns each year, thus providing a rich talent pipeline for the future.

Ms Cook says: 'Global nomads exist primarily within the divisions rather than being based at the centre and being posted out. The nomads are those whom the organization can send to any market, who connect quickly, are open and inquisitive, and ask a lot of questions at a high level and at grass roots. They build a local strategy and business by combining what they know has worked but with a keen sense of the local market, to create a compelling new offering.'

The company continues to see Europe and Asia as growth markets. In markets like India, the company notes there is a growing middle class with growing aspirations, and a healthy economy. The company also continues to believe the Chinese market will be an opportunity over time as it evolves.

News Corp also sees opportunities in Europe, as evidenced in its efforts since 2003 to build Sky Italia into a pay television powerhouse and valued brand, and its more recent investment in Sky Deutschland in Germany.

The company has looked not only at geographic opportunities, but also at the future to anticipate changes in what consumers and employees will want.

It has looked at generational changes including Generation Y, the development of the multi-generational workforce, and the changing nature of 'work'.

As a creative company that relies on attracting the best talent to create, package and distribute content, they know they must stay ahead of change.

In the past three years, the company started to implement initiatives designed to evolve a 'flexible, durable organization'.

The ageing population, Baby Boomers, parents, Generation Y and the new 'dream generation' are all interested in a more balanced life, and Ms Cook notes that the economic recession also gave pause for thought:

> The job market has been tough and people have tended to move less, due to fears of job stability. But the economic recession has also caused many people to stop and re-evaluate the notion of jobs for life, and financial security. You hear about things like the 'slow' movement in Europe, where people are reappraising a lifestyle of heavy consumerism and personal wealth creation, and seeking to simplify their lives and needs.
>
> The notion of work, and a job for life, is being questioned, and we need to think ahead about what that might mean for employers.
>
> For creative people, and the next generation, of course they'll need to earn a living, but they may not want to work in the same way as the Baby Boomers. So we need to think about how we get the most creative people to want to 'work' with us – whether it's as an employee or an independent contractor or part of what we call a 'virtual Velcro team' – who come together for an exciting project, then pull apart. And this could include a range of people from young creatives to part-timers and 'retired' experts.
>
> At News Corp we think in really flexible, diverse ways, so we never assume there's only one right way to do anything. So we use any combination – global nomads, Velcro project teams and virtual groups collaborating through technology – to create more diversity of thought. You don't just get the same group of people with the same thought patterns of how things should work.
>
> We're not known for treading the same path as others, and we always challenge the way things are done to make them better.
>
> The success of global nomads as culture infusers, and changes in technology, mean that both mobility and virtual connection will shape the future of work.

Our nomads provide the glue and enable us to leverage on the ground in new businesses and markets, and this next generation of creative workers want to be able to work in flexible, connected ways from anywhere, anytime, including in virtual teams.

To enable this, about 18 months ago the company launched a global collaboration platform called 'OurNews', which now has 16,000 employees worldwide on it. These people can connect, search for expertise, join or form groups, and share content and collaborate. The take-up has been rapid, and provides a natural transition for people used to connecting outside through social networking to do the same inside but with the focus on business and innovation.

Although we're a big business, we know it's imperative for our talent that we provide a work experience that's personalized and connected, where people feel they can be a part of something big and global. They need to feel they can make a difference regardless of their role or location or age or preferred way of working.

Companies say 'People are a valuable asset.' We say 'People are our competitive edge.'

Rita Vanhauwenhusyse, Global Talent Adviser, Rio Tinto plc

Rio Tinto is a leading international business involved in each stage of metal and mineral production. It produces aluminium, copper, diamonds, coal, iron ore, uranium, gold and industrial minerals such as borates. Production is mainly centred in Australia and North America but operations cover over 50 countries. The organization employs around 106,000 people.

The past two years have seen significant changes as the company has had to deal with a series of external challenges. This has meant changes in decisions, which in turn have created concern and anxiety, but there has been a sense that the organization can work its way through these challenges to maintain a sustainable business. This has generated a high level of pride and a strong upbeat mood with the recovery of trade, especially with China and India. Whilst these have been major markets for a number of years, the recovery has meant Rio Tinto is very focused on the developing and emerging markets including Eastern Russia and Africa.

The big people issue is where to find the right talent today and to start building leadership and professional pipelines for the next 10 years. As the current workforce is ageing, the need to address mobility and attrition has become a major priority. The hunt for talent for these new markets has meant that the company is having to be more innovative in looking for key talents – not from traditional sources. The emerging markets such as Africa and Russia pose a more complex set of challenges – not least remoteness, language, culture and security.

The second major talent issue is around future leadership skills which have traditionally been reliant on long-serving, loyal mining engineers and geologists but now need a new set of capabilities: cultural sensitivity, global sustainability and being able to deal with increasing regulation. Mobility is being factored in earlier as a way of attracting more talent into the organization, giving individuals more preference but at the same time giving the organization an opportunity to test out individuals.

A formal, integrated talent management process is being implemented for professional groups alongside a revamped performance management system. The yearly performance review process sets out objectives but also captures the personal profile and mobility status of individuals. Managers assess the ability of the employee to perform at the next level or above. These assessments go forward to the group's talent process, which then reviews performance against potential so that the ExecCo (top management team) gets insight of the top talent at that moment. In theory the top 600 are owned and deployed by this executive group; the reality remains a little different, but these are early days requiring further cultural change and business buy-in.

Ms Vanhauwenhusyse says:

> Today's talent is more cautious and Rio Tinto's credentials of tradition and sustainability, combined with the opportunity to travel, are attractive to a wider group of young professionals in the traditional operating markets.
>
> However, in certain markets such as India, attraction and retention are more challenging, where the rising economy places emphasis on employability rather than career development.
>
> The organization has many staff with between 15 and 20 years' experience, with incredible technical know-how and operational knowledge but who lack the adaptability and agility demanded by the new world. The company needs a better balance to combine this experience with the dynamism of the nomads to ensure effective knowledge transfer and to build greater diversity and multiculturalism.
>
> The key is to anticipate the future and reap the current learning.

Fredrico Wright, Corporate HR, Remuneration and Benefits Manager, Petrobras

Petrobras is Brazil's largest company and its main flagship organization. It is the fourth biggest energy company in the world with a market value of over US$ 160 billion and has been rated as the world's fourth placed 'most respected company'. The organization has a global presence in 28 countries, producing over 2 million barrels of oil and over 425,000 barrels of natural gas daily. Besides the main activity of exploration, extraction, refining and transportation of oil and natural gas, the company has invested heavily in developing biocombustible fuels such as ethanol, seeking partnerships with other international organizations. Today this division produces over 170 million litres of biodiesel per year, with feedstock coming from primarily family farms in Brazil.

The holding company employs 76,000 people worldwide across 28 countries, of whom 56,000 are in Brazil. Growth has mainly been in Brazil due to discovery of oilfields situated in deep and ultra-deep waters off the coast. They also have some major operations in the Gulf of Mexico, Argentina, Angola and Japan.

Petrobras is driven by the challenge of supplying the energy that propels development and ensures the future of Brazilian society, underpinned with values of technical competency, ethics, cordiality and a respect of diversity.

Although publically traded, the business's major shareholder is the government of Brazil. The company performs as an energy company with businesses that search for oil in the depths of the sea. The corporate strategy is to integrate growth, profitability and socio-environmental responsibility.

Its 2020 mission and vision are to deliver performance 'transparently and with attentive eyes on what is going on in Brazil and in the world'. Its mission is to 'operate in a safe and profitable manner in Brazil and abroad, with social and environmental responsibility, providing products and services that meet client needs and that contribute to the development of Brazil and the countries in which Petrobras operates'. Its vision is that it will be 'one of the five largest integrated energy companies in the world and the preferred choice among our stakeholders'.

There are 10 corporate values as follows:

Sustainable development. We pursue business success under a long-term perspective, contributing to economic and social development and to a healthy environment in the communities where we have operations.

Integration. We seek to maximize collaboration and to seize synergies among teams, areas and units, ensuring an integrated vision of the company in our actions and decisions.

Results. We seek continuously to generate value for all stakeholders, focusing on capital discipline and cost management. We value and acknowledge, in a differentiated manner, high-performance people and teams.

Readiness for change. We are ready for change and accept the responsibility for inspiring and creating positive change.

Entrepreneurship and innovation. We cultivate the overcoming of challenges and risk and seek, relentlessly, to generate and implement innovative technological and business solutions that help Petrobras systems's ethical principles.

Ethics and transparency. Our business, actions, commitments and other relationships are guided by Petrobras System's ethical principles.

Respect for life. We respect life in all of its forms, expressions and situations, and seek excellence in matters that involve health, safety and the environment.

Human and cultural diversity. We value human and cultural diversity in our relationships with people and institutions. We ensure the principles of respect for difference, non-discrimination and equal opportunities.

People. We turn people and their development into a performance differential of Petrobras.

Proud to be Petrobras. We are proud to belong to a Brazilian company that makes a difference no matter where it operates, for its history, achievements, and its capacity to overcome challenges.

As described in Chapter 6, these are expressed as very different values from established mature market multinationals, notably the respect of life, people and pride, the latter being the most notable difference in both statement and behaviour in the new world.

Petrobras has been growing steady and continuously for many years but this will accelerate in the next 10 as the corporate strategy looks to double exploration by 2020. The organization also has some 30 years' experience in biofuels such as ethanol, petrochemical, natural gas and thermal factories. The oil and gas sectors need larger workforces, so Petrobras, like others, will be looking to attract new talent from outside Brazil, and the number of expats is likely to rise in the next three to five years.

As Petrobras is a half-public and half-private firm, hiring new employees has a specific application process with many tests. Most new recruits will come from Brazil, but foreign workers can be placed on the payroll. The company, however, works with many partners in joint ventures, such as Chevron, British Gas, Shell and Galp. Petrobras will count on other workers typically from Columbia, Bolivia and Venezuela. However, these people are considered 'rotators' who come to Brazil for a while because they can never be permanent and can never localize.

As to the workforce of the future, the company does not expect the skill base to change significantly in the next few years, although technology will help explore more remote areas. At present the company operates a more traditional expat model, with Brazilians being sent away for two to four years before returning to Brazil, given the local regulations. Today there are some 200 expats, with a full range of roles from general managers (local CEOs) to technicians, as needs require. Most are senior experienced workers.

Karen Beyer, Global Mobility Manager, GE

GE is a global infrastructure, finance and media company manufacturing items from everyday light bulbs to fuel cell technology. Its bywords are innovation and 'imagination at work'. The breadth of its services stretches from day-to-day appliances to being the world's leading producer of jet engines and rail technology; from energy, water treatment and electrical distribution to media and entertainment via NBC Universal. GE Capital and Commercial Services provide credit, loans, leasing and commercial insurance. Its operates in over 160 countries.

The company is renowned for its culture based on strong vision, passion and a drive to make a difference in the world. It has established a high-performance culture that emphasizes high integrity with energy. The GE Foundation combines philanthropy with volunteerism to impact the communities where it does business.

GE prides itself on being able to invest and grow its workforce by offering opportunities throughout the world, acting as a talent magnet to give people 'some of the most exciting and dynamic challenges of a lifetime'.

Since the financial crisis, the organization has pulled back on its use of expats. It is re-examining and reducing the number of expatriate packages and instead favouring the use of shorter-term assignments through a more methodical, smarter process. It has a broad company-wide policy framework but looks to local market comparisons on a case-by-case basis. Previous arrangements tend to be driven by individuals and the business demands – now there is a clear talent review and a business case required.

The pattern of assignments is changing. There are fewer movements to cities like London or Tokyo and more to the emerging markets such as Nigeria where the organization is creating new businesses. More of these individuals are first-time expats on shorter assignments, typically project managers without families or without families accompanying them. In the mature markets such as Europe, there are a growing number of 'commuters' living in one country like Belgium but working on a weekly basis in another such as France. There is a sense in the current climate that individuals are willing to make big sacrifices in the short term but this may not last.

GE as described above has a good reputation for development, providing challenging roles and management opportunities early on in individual careers. It is understood that global moves are an important input to ensure that the organization continues to build a global talent pipeline. There is more talent segmentation occurring but this is more at business level rather than at a corporate level.

For the future the company is seeing a mixed pattern of recovery across the world and at present this has not created skill gaps since whilst some business markets are opening up, others are shrinking or closing. All of which is making the role of managing global mobility more challenging as each situation requires more personal attention.

As for the younger generation coming into the workforce, Ms Beyer does recognize that many have extensive travel experience and are more confident. The company culture is very strong and focused on local markets in both what it says and does. At present the expansion into emerging markets has not presented significant problems – it has a strong record of working with diverse communities. Returning expats are less of an issue as the company is big enough to find suitable challenging roles for them.

INDEX

NB: page numbers in *italic* indicate figures or tables